Men with Adult ADHD

Highly Effective Techniques for
Mastering Focus, Time Management,
and Overcoming Anxiety

Thomas West

sources. Please consult a licensed professional before attempting any techniques outlined in this book.

By reading this document, the reader agrees that under no circumstances is the author responsible for any losses, direct or indirect, which are incurred as a result of the use of the information contained within this document, including, but not limited to, — errors, omissions, or inaccuracies.

Table of Contents

Introduction

Mark jolted awake to the shrill sound of his alarm, groggy but already dreading the chaotic search for his socks. His morning routine was a scavenger hunt, with one sock tangled in the pile of clothes on his bed and the other inexplicably in the kitchen, atop another heap of laundry. He sighed, knowing that the day had just begun, and shuffled past his desk, a veritable graveyard of empty water bottles. There, amidst the clutter, he spotted a mug filled with yesterday's coffee. Already falling behind, he took a few bitter sips of the cold, stale brew and hurried out the door.

At work, a mountain of unopened emails greeted him, a sight that had become all too familiar. His laptop screen was a chaotic mess of over thirty open tabs, each a reminder of the tasks he had yet to complete. A meeting was scheduled for the morning, but half an hour in, Mark's mind wandered. He couldn't remember the instructions given to him, drowned out by a catchy tune playing on a loop in his head. The pressure of looming deadlines bore down on him, and he tried to juggle multiple tasks, only to lose track whenever he picked up his phone. "Just for a few seconds," he always told himself. Still, fifteen minutes later, he'd be lost in the labyrinth of social media.

Unable to sit a second longer, he visited a colleague, seeking a brief respite from the mounting stress. Back at his desk, he struggled to refocus, overwhelmed by the ticking clock and the tasks that seemed to multiply by the minute. After work, Mark planned to unwind with friends, but first, he needed to stop by home to walk his dog. This simple errand turned into an hour-long conversation with his neighbor. His initial ten-minute plan was dissolving into the evening. When he arrived at the restaurant, his friends had already started dinner. He slipped into his seat, feeling the familiar pang of being unheard and the sting of their frustrated looks and frequent shushes.

Mark's life was a whirlwind of distractions and missed opportunities. Each day, he struggled to keep up with the demands of his work and personal life. Yet, amidst the chaos, a part of him yearned for a semblance of order and a chance to truly connect with those around him. He knew he needed to change, to find a way to manage his time and attention better, but the path to that change seemed as elusive as the second sock each morning.

Does any of this sound familiar? If you're a man living with ADHD, you are not alone. Many men face the same daily battles.

ADHD is often perceived as a childhood disorder, something that one might outgrow with age. However, many men carry these symptoms into adulthood, struggling to maintain social approval, professional success, and personal relationships. Society's expectations of men - to be strong, focused, and reliable - only add to the weight of this invisible burden. For men with ADHD, these expectations can feel like an impossible challenge. In a world that values conformity and consistency, men with ADHD often find themselves on the periphery, fighting for acceptance. They are judged for their restlessness, their perceived inattentiveness, and their impulsive decisions. This constant scrutiny leads to a persistent feeling of inadequacy. They question their self-worth and worry that they will never meet societal standards. A staggering statistic reveals that approximately 6.7% of adults in the World have ADHD, and many of them are undiagnosed (Attention Deficit Disorder Association). This means millions of men are navigating life without understanding why they struggle in ways others don't. They often blame themselves for their shortcomings, unaware that a legitimate condition underlies their daily battles.

I wrote *Men with Adult ADHD* as a vital part of my journey to overcome the daily challenges of living with ADHD. I spent thousands of hours learning from experts and diving into scientific articles. This extensive research and personal experience taught me practical techniques to calm anxious thoughts, master emotions, and sharpen focus.

You picked up *Men with Adult ADHD* because you, or someone you care about, might be experiencing these very struggles. And let me assure you, it was the right decision. Understanding ADHD in men is the first step toward managing it effectively. This book is not just about identifying symptoms or offering generic advice. It's about diving deep into the lived experiences of men who face this daily challenge. It's about providing practical strategies grounded in the latest research to help you or your loved ones navigate this complex landscape. Reading this book can be a transformative experience; it offers insights into why certain behaviors occur and how to manage them. This is a journey towards self-acceptance, improved relationships, and professional success. It's about breaking free from the chains of societal expectations and redefining what it means to be a man with ADHD.

Here are the key benefits you can expect from reading this book:

- Learn how ADHD affects men differently and find better ways to handle these challenges.

- Discover the most common misconceptions about ADHD and learn effective solutions rooted in its true nature.

- Discover tips to control impulsive spending and keep your finances in order for a more stable future.

- Improve your relationships by understanding how ADHD affects your interactions and learning better communication skills.

- Boost your job performance by recognizing ADHD-related issues and using strategies to overcome them.

- Declutter your home and digital space.

- Use the 6-week CBT program to support executive functions.

The book's first part aims to uncover the real nature of ADHD. It challenges common misconceptions that risk boosting the stigma and approaching ADHD with the wrong mindset. The second part delves deep into the science that explains how ADHD affects the brain. It continues by providing various science-based solutions that can improve ADHD symptoms. In the third part, we address daily obstacles men with ADHD face and practical solutions to overcome them. The fourth part delivers a training program to support and boost productivity, time management, planning, and more.

As you turn the page, I encourage you to keep an open mind and a compassionate heart. Whether you are reading this for yourself or to support someone you care about, know that you are not alone. The journey through these pages will equip you with the understanding and strategies needed to navigate the complexities of ADHD. Let this book be your guide as you explore the intricacies of living with ADHD as a man. It's a step toward managing the condition and thriving despite it. You will find stories that resonate, advice that empowers, and strategies that transform. Your journey to understanding and embracing Adult ADHD starts here.

PART 1

Dispelling Stigma and
Misconceptions

Chapter 1: Uncovering Causes and Gaining Clarity

"We use amphetamines to conveniently modify the behavior of bored boys." - Jordan Peterson

The question of whether ADHD is a legitimate condition has been hotly debated. Renowned psychologist Jordan Peterson argues vehemently against the widespread acceptance of ADHD. He posits that ADHD is not an actual disease; it's an excuse for poor behavior. According to Peterson, the rise in ADHD diagnoses is a result of societal changes that no longer tolerate the natural variations in children's behavior, particularly boys.

On a similar note, Gabor Maté, a physician known for his work in addiction, stress, and childhood development, focuses on the role of trauma in the manifestation of ADHD.

"I didn't buy into the medical mantra that this is a genetic disease."

Maté asserts that environmental stressors and early childhood experiences significantly shape the presentation of ADHD symptoms. He challenges the notion that ADHD is mainly genetic, emphasizing the importance of understanding the trauma experienced to comprehend someone's struggles.

The debate is fueled further by the statistics, which indicate a significant increase in ADHD diagnoses over the past few decades:

- The prevalence of ADHD in children aged 4 to 17 in the U.S. increased from around 6% in the 1990s to approximately 10% by 2016.

- Between 2007 and 2016, the prevalence of ADHD in adults more than doubled.

- It is estimated that 366 million adults are currently living with ADHD.

(CHADD & NIMH)

While Peterson and Maté are highly respected in their fields, their expertise in ADHD specifically is limited. While valuable, Peterson's focus on behavioral psychology and Maté's emphasis on trauma do not encompass the full spectrum of ADHD research. Their perspectives, though influential, often overshadow the voices of those who have dedicated their careers to studying ADHD.

A single voice stood out, ringing loud and clear. Dr. Russell Barkley is a preeminent clinical psychologist whose extensive research on ADHD has created more than 300 scientific articles on the disorder. He has over 40 years of research experience, specifically on ADHD, and his clinical work has impacted thousands of patients. Barkley's research starkly contrasts the views of Peterson and Maté, and he didn't hesitate to confront them online. His opinions on Maté's and Peterson's ideas can be summarized as "nonsense on stilts" and "pathetic scholarship." He emphasizes that understanding the genetic basis of ADHD is crucial for effective treatment and management. His findings underscore the importance of early diagnosis and intervention, which can drastically improve the quality of life for those affected.

THE TRUE ORIGIN OF ADHD

Could ADHD be a legacy passed down through generations, or is it a consequence of our ever-changing surroundings?

This question has puzzled scientists, doctors, and parents for decades. While exploring this complex issue, you will enter a hidden world where genes and environment compete for significance. Imagine a delicate plant struggling to grow in rocky soil. Such conditions can stunt its growth, as early life complications impact brain development. Environmental influences play a crucial role in the development of ADHD. Environmental factors account for approximately 10-15% of the variation in ADHD symptoms (Froehlich et al., 2011; Kadlaskar et al., 2023). Factors include:

- exposure to alcohol during pregnancy
- pregnancy complications
- low birth weight
- head trauma

For instance, premature birth and low birth weight correlate to a 35-45% increased risk of developing ADHD (Froehlich et al.,

2011). Children exposed to alcohol in utero are about 2.5 times more likely to develop the disorder compared to those whose mothers abstained (Kadlaskar et al., 2023). These environmental factors are significant; however, nothing compares to the influence of genetics.

The role of genetics is pivotal in ADHD, accounting for 70-80% of its variance. Such statistics make ADHD one of the most genetically influenced psychiatric disorders. Picture your genes as a deck of cards shuffled and dealt to you at birth. When a parent has ADHD, their deck includes a card that increases the likelihood of ADHD. Consequently, their child is eight times more likely to develop the disorder compared to peers without an ADHD-affected parent. Also, older parents should consider de novo mutations. These are new and not inherited from either parent. Such mutations are more common in children born to older parents. Parents who wait until they are 30 or older to have children have eight to ten times more mutations in their eggs and sperm compared to younger parents. Such genetic alterations can contribute to ADHD, even in families with no previous history of the disorder. It is like adding a new wildcard to the genetic deck, randomly altering the outcome (Kadlaskar et al., 2023).

On the other hand, as we explained, many prominent figures fight this proposition. They emphasize the role of childhood trauma in the development of ADHD, suggesting that early emotional distress and unstable environments disrupt neurological development. Maté, for example, contends that the child's nurturing context overshadows genetic predispositions.

Who should you listen to?

Twin studies, considered the most compelling proof in genetic research, offer profound insights. These studies compare identical twins, who share 100% of their genes, with fraternal twins, who share about 50%. If identical twins, nature's perfect clones, show higher ADHD rates than fraternal twins, then genetics have a strong influence. Concordance rates for ADHD in identical twins are strikingly high. Identical twins share the trait 75-90% of the time. In contrast, fraternal twins show much lower rates, between 30 and 40% (Faraone & Doyle, 2001; Nikolas & Burt, 2010). Such stark contrast highlights the solid genetic component of ADHD (Faraone & Larsson, 2019).

While the debate rages on, it is essential to acknowledge that both sides might hold elements of truth. Misdiagnosis is a legitimate concern. Overlapping symptoms with other conditions, societal pressures, and lack of comprehensive evaluations can lead to incorrect diagnoses.

In Part 2, you will learn to prevent misdiagnoses and customize a solution that fits your unique situation.

But first, let's answer one of the most popular questions surrounding ADHD. Were traits often seen in ADHD, like impulsivity, essential for survival in ancient times?

TAKEAWAYS

1. **ADHD's Genetic Foundation:** Twin studies reveal that ADHD has a strong genetic basis. This highlights that ADHD is not mainly a result of environmental factors but is deeply rooted in our genetic makeup.

2. **Challenges of Misdiagnosis:** ADHD is often misdiagnosed because its symptoms overlap with those of other disorders. Understanding this overlap is crucial for accurate diagnosis and effective treatment.

3. **Global Prevalence of ADHD:** Despite common misconceptions, ADHD affects more than 366 million adults globally. This demonstrates that ADHD is a widespread condition that transcends cultural and geographic boundaries.

Chapter 2: Navigating ADHD with a Growth-Oriented Mindset

Imagine a hunter in a vast and untamed wilderness, moving with a restless energy that sets him apart from his peers. His sharp senses and impulsive decisions become his most significant assets in the hunt. While others methodically plan their moves, he instinctively reacts to the slightest rustle in the underbrush, his mind always alert and scanning for opportunities. His unpredictable patterns confuse and outmaneuver prey that would otherwise evade a more predictable pursuer.

Upon his return to the village, laden with the spoils of the hunt, he is met with admiration and respect. The tribe gathers around, their eyes wide with awe as they examine the bounty he has secured. Elders nod approvingly, recognizing the skill and bravery required to achieve such a feat. Children look up to him with shining eyes, inspired by his prowess. Around the communal fire that night, stories of his hunt are recounted with reverence, his name mentioned with a newfound respect. His once-misunderstood energy and impulsiveness are now celebrated as the very qualities that ensured the tribe's survival and prosperity. Through the hunt, he has earned a place of honor and demonstrated that his unique way of interacting with the world can lead to extraordinary success.

Thom Hartmann would love this story. Hartmann is an American psychotherapist who popularized the "Hunter vs. Farmer" theory. He suggests that individuals with ADHD have traits that would benefit hunters in the past. Heightened alertness and impulsivity are traits supposedly beneficial in tracking and capturing prey. On the other hand, the "farmer" traits include patience, the ability to focus on repetitive tasks, and long-term planning, which are beneficial in an agricultural society.

Hartmann argues that modern society, with its structured environments like classrooms and offices, is more suited to "farmer" traits, leading to the perception that ADHD traits are problematic. He suggests that ADHD should be viewed as a difference rather than a disorder (Hartmann, 2019). With a shift to warriors, Peter S. Jensen promoted a similar idea. Peter S. Jensen, M.D., is a renowned child and adolescent psychiatrist and suggested that ADHD traits were advantageous in combat situations. Both Hartmann and Jensen support the long-romanticized idea that ADHD traits were advantageous in humanity's past. They suggest that these characteristics were once a superpower for hunting or warfare. This adaptationist perspective posits that ADHD must have been adaptive somehow, contributing to survival and success in ancient human societies.

But was it truly an advantage?

In a groundbreaking study, researchers led by Esteller-Cucala set out to explore the evolutionary history of ADHD. They aimed to understand how natural selection has influenced the prevalence of ADHD-related genes over thousands of years. The team analyzed ancient DNA samples. Ranging from 45,000 years ago to the present, they tracked the changes in these genetic markers. The data was extensive, including ancient human remains from various periods and regions (Esteller-Cucala et al., 2020). They wanted to find out if ADHD traits were helpful or harmful to early humans in their environments. By examining these ancient genomes, the researchers identified how common ADHD-related genes were in different populations and times.

The findings were striking. The study revealed that these genes were more common in ancient populations, indicating that ADHD traits were more prevalent in early human environments. However, even during the hunter-gatherer era, the environment was not entirely favorable to these traits. The frequency of ADHD-related genes started to decline even before the advent of agriculture, suggesting that these traits were becoming less advantageous well before humans began farming.

This research shows that ADHD is not a result of modern technology and our fast-paced lifestyle. Most importantly, ADHD is not a superpower or a gift. It's not just a quirk; it's a disorder that has negatively impacted the lives of millions of people. However, it is not a life sentence. A proper diagnosis doesn't mean you are broken; quite the opposite. It brings an understanding of past struggles and can shift your mindset to take on the challenge with the proper knowledge. Many men with ADHD thrived thanks to accurate treatment and management.

That's right, not only survive but also thrive. ADHD presents challenges but also an opportunity. The opportunity to build character. As Helen Keller said, "Character cannot be developed in ease and quiet. Only through experience of trial and suffering can the soul be strengthened, ambition inspired, and success achieved." Managing ADHD involves navigating significant challenges, but these trials can pave the way for success. By embracing and overcoming the difficulties of ADHD, you will transform adversity into a powerful source of growth and achievement.

In Week 1 of Part 4 training, you will receive tools to help you accept your diagnosis and quickly move on to a fulfilling life. In the meantime, let's focus on learning. Understanding the intricacies of ADHD is the first step toward turning its challenges into opportunities for personal and professional growth.

Then, what is ADHD?

TAKEAWAYS

1. **ADHD Traits and History:** Typical ADHD traits like impulsivity appear to have been present and inefficient even before the advent of farming. This suggests that ADHD is not merely a result of modern technology and our fast-paced lifestyle.

2. **ADHD Mindset:** If you have ADHD, don't see yourself as a victim. Instead, view it as a challenge and an opportunity to build character. Many people have built resilience and thrived with ADHD.

Chapter 3: Why ADHD Issues in Men Don't Fit the Standard Narrative

Imagine walking in a park. You see a small child, face flushed red, tears streaming down his cheeks, screaming in frustration while desperately kicking a tree. You think, "Kids will be kids." Now, picture the same scene, but the child is a teenager. You might feel a pang of empathy, recalling your turbulent teenage years and the whirlwind of emotions that came with them. But now, imagine a 35-year-old man in the park, screaming and kicking that same tree. Suddenly, it's not just a tantrum—it's unsettling. Your reaction shifts from understanding to concern.

Why do you react so differently?

Because age matters in evaluating behavior, and understanding this is crucial when it comes to ADHD.

HOW ADHD STANDARDS DON'T WORK FOR MEN

ADHD is a developmental disorder. It indicates a slower progression in specific neuropsychological functions compared to typical development within the same age group. Most kids start speaking their first words around age one. By age 7, they can read simple books, write down their names, and do basic math. ADHD slows development, and toddlers take longer to absorb skills and behaviors. It's a quantitative problem, not a qualitative one. This means it's about the degree or amount of ability rather than a different type of ability. Think of it like running a race. Everyone runs the same path, but someone with a developmental disorder runs slower and faces more obstacles. They can do the same things but at a different pace or with more difficulty.

Now that we have made clear how ADHD relates to age-inappropriate behaviors, at what age does it go away?

When you catch a cold, you experience a sore throat and runny nose and feel tired for a little while. It's annoying and hard to focus or enjoy your day, but you know it will disappear in a week or two. Unfortunately, ADHD is like a shadow; it will follow into adulthood. It's a chronic issue that goes underdiagnosed. Criteria for ADHD were initially developed for children, and it seems that only a tiny percentage of adults are correctly diagnosed. Dr. Andrew J. Cutler, a leading expert in ADHD and psychiatry, has highlighted that up to 80% of adults with ADHD remain undiagnosed, leaving millions unaware of their condition (Cutler, 2022).

Why is it bad?

Because they go untreated, and the consequences are catastrophic. Beyond the daily struggles, there is a darker, often overlooked consequence of this condition. A comprehensive study published in BMC Psychiatry followed individuals from birth to age 46, uncovering a sobering statistic. Adults with ADHD are four times more likely to die significantly earlier than individuals without the disorder (Dalsgaard et al., 2015).

This study delves deep into the lives of those with ADHD. It reveals that the challenges faced extend far beyond academic or professional difficulties. It shows that the essence of existence—safety, health, and life expectancy—is at stake. This revelation can be heart-wrenching, but learning about the heightened risk of early mortality adds a layer of fear and urgency. To prevent further tragedies, we need to delve deeper into the nature of ADHD. In the following chapters, you will discover solutions that have helped millions of men with ADHD. However, you won't be able to apply them if you first don't understand the fundamental nature of ADHD. Therefore, let's explore the standard psychological view and why it's far from perfect.

18 SYMPTOMS THAT FAIL TO PAINT THE FULL PICTURE

ADHD stands for Attention-Deficit/Hyperactivity Disorder. It is a neurodevelopmental disorder characterized by persistent inattention, hyperactivity, and impulsivity that interfere with development. The DSM-5 (Diagnostic and Statistical Manual of Mental Disorders), the standard diagnostic manual used by mental health professionals, categorizes ADHD into three presentations:

1. Predominantly inattentive

2. Predominantly hyperactive-impulsive

3. Combined presentation

The DSM can be compared to a comprehensive "instruction manual" for the mind, much like a detailed cookbook for mental health professionals. Picture the recipes as the disorders and symptoms as the ingredients. Let's look at the ingredients first.

Hyperactivity – Impulsivity

To be diagnosed with the hyperactive-impulsive presentation, an individual must exhibit often at least five of the following symptoms:

1. Appears restless, moving hands, feet, or shifting in their seat.
2. Leaves their seat in situations when remaining seated is expected.
3. Moves around or climbs in situations where it's inappropriate, showing a need for physical activity.
4. Struggles to engage in quiet, calm activities or play.
5. Seems to be in constant motion, described as having an "on the go" attitude.
6. Talks excessively, with continuous speech.
7. Blurts out answers before questions are completed, interrupting conversations.
8. Has difficulty waiting for their turn, displaying impatience.
9. Intrudes on others, interrupting conversations or taking over group activities.

(American Psychiatric Association, 2013)

Inattention

For the Inattention presentation, the individual must exhibit often at least five of the following symptoms:

1. Overlooks details or makes careless mistakes in tasks or activities.
2. Has difficulty maintaining focus on tasks or activities, such as reading or listening during conversations.
3. Does not seem to pay attention when spoken to directly, as if their mind is elsewhere.
4. Struggles to follow through on instructions, leaving tasks unfinished.
5. Has difficulty organizing tasks and activities, leading to disorganization.
6. Avoids or dislikes tasks that require sustained mental effort, like homework or reading.
7. Misplaces items needed for tasks, such as keys, paperwork, or school materials.
8. Is easily sidetracked by unrelated thoughts or external stimuli.
9. Forgetful in daily routines, like missing appointments or neglecting chores.

(American Psychiatric Association, 2013)

Furthermore, the symptoms must be pervasive, significant, and persistent and have originated during childhood or adolescence (see Takeaways).

Now that we have all the ingredients, we can create the recipe.

- Predominantly Inattentive Presentation: Characterized by at least five symptoms of inattention and fewer than five symptoms of hyperactivity-impulsivity.

- Predominantly Hyperactive-Impulsive Presentation: Identified by at least five symptoms of hyperactivity-impulsivity and fewer than five symptoms of inattention.

- Combined Presentation: Diagnosed when an individual exhibits at least five symptoms of inattention and at least five symptoms of hyperactivity-impulsivity.

Before you self-diagnose, it's crucial to understand that these criteria are just a starting point. While the DSM provides some indication, ADHD experts, like Dr. Thomas E. Brown, have criticized the DSM-5 for its narrow definition of symptoms. He emphasizes that ADHD involves more than just inattention and hyperactivity. Therefore, the aspects considered so far fail to show the fundamental nature of the problem and consequently support the best strategies to solve it. ADHD symptoms are like the ripples on the surface of a pond. They are the visible signs of a more profound, complex disturbance beneath the water. Therefore, to truly grasp the nature of ADHD, we need to delve deeper into the underlying factors that drive these behaviors.

ADHD IS NOT AN ATTENTION DEFICIT DISORDER

Attention is often oversimplified. Instead, it's a complex mental function. There are many types of attention, such as sustained attention, selective attention, divided attention, and arousal. For example, the ability to stay alert and respond quickly to things isn't always affected by ADHD. Many people with ADHD are alert and responsive in exciting or new situations. Therefore, calling ADHD an "attention disorder" is misleading. Conversely, ADHD often causes difficulties with sustained attention. Therefore, it can be challenging in classrooms or workplaces, where you must concentrate for extended periods. Also, focusing on one task while ignoring distractions, known as selective attention, is a big challenge.

Hyperactivity is also misleading. In children, hyperactivity often shows as constant movement, fidgeting, and an inability to sit still, which disrupt activities and social interactions. However, as ADHD transitions into adulthood, the hyperactivity usually fades. The main issue shifts from physical restlessness to verbal and cognitive control. This is why ADHD diagnoses do not translate well to adults.

Then, if ADHD in adults is neither an issue of hyperactivity nor inattention, what is the real nature of the challenges?

TAKEAWAYS

1. **Core Understanding:** ADHD's true nature extends beyond attention deficits and hyperactivity. It involves a complex interplay of cognitive functions and behavioral patterns.

2. **Neurodevelopmental Basis:** ADHD is fundamentally a neurodevelopmental disorder, meaning it originates from atypical brain development. Recognizing this helps in developing the best solutions.

3. **Early Onset:** Symptoms must have originated during childhood or adolescence, indicating the early onset of the disorder.

4. **Pervasiveness:** Symptoms must be present across multiple settings, including work, personal life, social settings, and financial management, showing a broad impact.

5. **Significant Impairment:** The symptoms must cause substantial impairment in major life activities, indicating that the individual is not functioning well.

6. **Persistence:** Symptoms must have been present for at least 6 months.

7. **Challenges in Adult Diagnosis:** The symptoms of ADHD, as outlined in the DSM, often don't translate well to adults, leading to many cases going undiagnosed. This highlights the need for more tailored diagnostic criteria for adults.

Chapter 4: ADHD's Effect on Six Executive Functions

During the long and brutal Marcomannic Wars, conditions for the Roman troops were far from easy. The military camps were harsh places, often set up in remote, rugged areas exposed to bad weather. The air smelled of damp earth and sweat, mixed with smoke from many campfires. Tents of rough fabric flapped in the wind, offering little protection from the cold and rain.

Despite his imperial status, Marcus Aurelius did not isolate himself from these conditions. He could have stayed in the comfort of Rome, but he chose to live with his men, sharing their discomforts. His tent was no different from his soldiers, and he endured the same cold, damp nights. His chronic illness added more suffering as he often had severe pain and extreme fatigue. Losing several of his children further tested the emperor's strength as it wasn't enough. These sad events weighed heavily on him, each death a blow to his already burdened heart. However, he stayed calm and assertive despite his pain, speaking to his men with encouraging and wise words. In his reflections, Aurelius thought about finding inner peace amidst external chaos. One clear example is how he handled peace talks with the Germanic tribes. Instead of wanting total conquest, he chose long-term stability over short-term glory. His steadfastness and shared suffering earned him his troops' deep respect and admiration.

Marcus Aurelius's superpower was his ability to self-regulate; he could consciously control his actions, thoughts, and emotions to achieve specific goals. He was masterful at setting goals, adjusting behaviors, and maintaining focus and motivation.

Unfortunately, ADHD betrays self-regulation. It disrupts the mechanisms that Marcus Aurelius exemplified, leading to a different life. A life resembling a fallen empire:

- The obesity rate in individuals with ADHD is 70% higher than in those without ADHD (Cortese & Vincenzi, 2016).
- 25% of substance abusers have ADHD (Van Emmerik-van Oortmerssen et al., 2012).
- 25% of prisoners have ADHD (Young et al., 2015).

Those pervasive numbers suggest that we are not simply dealing with an attention issue, and simplistic labels like "stupid" and "lazy" are not the smartest approach.

However, you don't have to be another statistic. By taking the time to read this book, you've chosen to prioritize your well-being. You are on the path to success. Together, we'll find practical ways to help you feel in control, leading to a life of outstanding achievements.

THE 6 KEY FUNCTIONS ADHD IMPACTS

The Cold War was at its peak, with the world anxiously watching as the United States and the Soviet Union clashed in a strategic battle. This was the backdrop for the 1972 World Chess Championship in Reykjavik, Iceland. Bobby Fischer from the United States challenged the reigning champion, Boris Spassky from the Soviet Union. The stakes were high: the world championship title and symbolic dominance during intense ideological rivalry. Fischer carefully planned his strategy, using bold moves and psychological tactics to outsmart and unsettle the experienced Spassky. He considered every possible move, anticipated his opponent's strategies, and adapted in real-time, changing the course of chess history. This strategic brilliance helped Fischer overcome the powerful Soviet chess machine, securing a decisive victory that made him one of the greatest chess players ever. Fischer's win in Reykjavik wasn't just luck or brute force; it showcased his exceptional mind.

The mental skills Fischer showed are based on what psychologists call executive functions. These mental processes help you manage your thoughts, actions, and emotions to reach your goals. They are like the hidden engines of your brain, helping you plan, focus, and remember instructions. These functions set us apart from other animals, giving us the brainpower to build civilizations, create art, and explore space. Neuroscientific research has pinpointed the specific brain region primarily responsible for these functions. This area is more developed in humans than other species, highlighting our unique cognitive capabilities. Functional MRI studies have shown that tasks involving planning, problem-solving, and decision-making activate this area, illustrating its crucial role in managing complex behaviors.

As you will learn in Chapter 5, this brain area is working inefficiently in men with ADHD. Because of that, six executive functions are compromised.

Executive functions are not a single entity but a collection of interrelated processes. Alvarez and Emory's (2006) research identifies critical components such as working memory, cognitive flexibility, and inhibitory control. Each component contributes uniquely to our ability to navigate complex environments and progress toward a goal. Progress toward a goal is the foundation of achievement. It requires movement from your situation to your desires. Unfortunately, ADHD stands on the path like a fallen tree after a storm.

Let's discover those six functions before uncovering solutions to improve them and increase brain efficacy.

1. SELF-AWARENESS

In September 1939, as World War II erupted, Slavomir Rawicz, a young Polish cavalry officer, was captured by the advancing Soviet Army. Accused of espionage, he was sentenced to 25 years of hard labor in a Siberian Gulag. This remote prison camp was notorious for its extreme cold, grueling labor, and near-starvation diet. Yet, Rawicz, driven by a fierce desire for freedom, began plotting his escape. By April 1941, they had enough. Rawicz and six other prisoners made a daring escape into the unknown Siberian wilderness. Their journey was marked by constant battles against the elements and the fear of recapture. They trekked through dense forests and across frozen rivers, always moving southward in hopes of reaching warmer climates. Without maps or compasses, they relied on the stars and their instincts to guide them. One of their greatest struggles was needing more feedback about their exact location and direction. Navigating through uncharted, hostile environments without reliable landmarks was a constant source of anxiety and danger.

Just as Rawicz and his companions struggled to know their physical location, individuals often grapple with understanding their internal state and direction in life. The absence of feedback on progress can lead to disorientation and frustration. In such situations, self-awareness becomes crucial. Like navigating without a map, understanding one's thoughts, feelings, and motivations requires introspection. Regular self-reflection helps individuals gain insight into their inner world, as Rawicz relied on his instincts and intuition to survive.

Self-awareness is the process of turning inward and understanding one's thoughts, emotions, and behaviors. It acts as a guiding compass, helping navigate the complexities of life with clarity and purpose by recognizing action patterns, understanding motivations, and aligning decisions with one's values. Self-awareness has three core components.

Emotional Recognition

Emotional recognition is at the heart of self-awareness—the capacity to identify and comprehend one's emotions. This skill goes beyond simply labeling feelings; it involves understanding their origins and implications.

Self-Reflection

"The unexamined life is not worth living."

The words of Socrates continue to resonate in today's era. Self-reflection is the mirror through which we view our past actions and thoughts, gaining insights that shape our future. Reflecting on our experiences enables a deeper understanding of ourselves, fostering personal growth and learning.

Self-Perception

Accurate self-perception is the lens through which we see our true selves—our strengths, weaknesses, and areas for growth. This trait is crucial for setting realistic goals and pursuing personal development.

Self-awareness is not an abstract, esoteric concept but a practical, everyday skill that enhances life's quality and depth. By recognizing your emotions, reflecting on your experiences, and maintaining an accurate self-view, you navigate the complexities of life with greater clarity and purpose. Self-awareness is the compass that will always point you toward your true north, guiding you through the labyrinth of existence with wisdom and grace.

Unfortunately, ADHD harms self-awareness. This impairment can make it difficult to recognize mistakes, understand your impact on others, or accurately assess your abilities and performance. Consequently, you may frequently encounter unexpected consequences or social missteps, leading to frustration and confusion. Over time, this persistent uncertainty and inability to predict or control outcomes can foster anxiety as you constantly grapple with the fear of unknown errors and the reactions they may provoke.

The first session of our 6-week training in Part 4 focuses on cultivating your self-awareness. In this session, you will explore the core components of self-awareness: emotional recognition, self-reflection, and accurate self-perception. Through guided introspection and practical exercises, you will learn to understand your thoughts, emotions, and behaviors, laying the foundation for your personal growth and enabling you to navigate life's complexities with greater clarity and purpose.

Let's now look at the second executive function impaired.

2. INHIBITION

A room full of preschool children, each faced with a single marshmallow. The task was deceptively simple: "resist eating the marshmallow for 15 minutes, and you will be rewarded with a second one". The Marshmallow Experiment, conducted by psychologist Walter Mischel in the late 1960s (Mischel et al., 1972), quickly became a hallmark study in self-control and delayed gratification. The children squirmed, sang songs, and even nibbled on the edges of their seats to avoid devouring the marshmallow. The scene was a mix of comedy and psychological torment, revealing profound truths about human behavior.

Inhibition, or self-restraint, is a complex concept essential to daily living. It involves the ability to hold back impulses, desires, or behaviors that could be harmful in the long term. Understanding inhibition requires exploring cognitive and behavioral control as well as moral and ethical considerations.

Cognitive and Behavioral Control

You are trying to focus on a complex task while your phone buzzes with notifications. This cognitive control closely relates to behavioral control, where you manage your actions to align with your goals. A classic example of cognitive and behavioral control in action is the concept of delay of gratification. The Marshmallow Experiment showed that children who couldn't wait for the second marshmallow had worse life outcomes than the children who could wait. They:

- scored lower on SATs (Mischel, Shoda, & Rodriguez, 1989)
- had higher body mass indices (Mischel, Shoda, & Rodriguez, 1989)

- exhibited more behavioral problems (Shoda, Mischel, & Peake, 1990)

This inability to delay gratification is a cornerstone of bad self-regulation (Baumeister & Heatherton, 1996).

Verbal inhibition is another critical area affected when you have ADHD. You might find yourself talking excessively and interrupting others, unable to suppress the urge to speak out of turn. This can lead to social and professional challenges, as the inability to control verbal output disrupts conversations and interactions. Unfortunately, it results in alienation from peers and colleagues.

Moreover, ADHD significantly impairs cognitive inhibition, the ability to suppress irrelevant thoughts and focus on the task at hand. This manifests as impulsive thinking, where you might struggle to filter out distractions and irrelevant thoughts, leading to hasty and often ill-considered decisions. This lack of cognitive control hinders your ability to plan and execute tasks that require sustained mental effort and foresight (Baumeister & Heatherton, 1996).

Moral and Ethical Considerations

Think of Jiminy Cricket from "Pinocchio"—the little voice of conscience that guides Pinocchio to make the right choices. Moral and ethical considerations are akin to having your own Jiminy Cricket. They influence our behavior by instilling a sense of right and wrong, empathy, and integrity.

The importance of moral and ethical considerations appears in various contexts. For instance, imagine you're at work, and you notice a colleague making a mistake on a project. You must decide whether to address the error and risk to cause tension or ignore it and let potential problems arise later. This internal moral compass is crucial for navigating complex social environments and making decisions that uphold societal values (Brown & Treviño, 2006).

When men have ADHD, the impact on inhibition begins early in childhood. Here, hyperactive and impulsive behaviors are often the first noticeable symptoms. These behaviors aren't just random bursts of energy; they signify a deeper struggle with controlling motor actions. This impulsivity leads to challenges in social interactions, such as difficulty waiting for your turn during play. It's no surprise if you haven't been invited to many sleepovers. This behavior can frustrate peers and hinder the formation of friendships, impacting self-esteem. While children exhibit restlessness and an inability to stay still, those traits often persist into adulthood in subtler forms, like a constant need to be busy.

In addition to motor, verbal, and cognitive inhibition, ADHD also impacts motivational and emotional self-regulation. These are crucial aspects of ADHD that require independent and in-depth discussion, so we dedicated an entire paragraph to them.

Since issues with inhibition are pervasive, Parts 3 and 4 of the book offer strategies for gaining control over your financial, professional, and love life.

In sum, ADHD's disruption of inhibition extends beyond mere hyperactivity or inattentiveness; it fundamentally impairs the executive functions that govern self-regulation. This impairment manifests across various domains—motor actions, verbal outputs, cognitive processes, motivational drives, and emotional responses—each contributing to the complex challenges you might experience daily (Baumeister & Heatherton, 1996; Moffitt et al., 2011; Duckworth & Seligman, 2005).

3. WORKING MEMORY

When was the last time you tried to remember a phone number long enough to dial it? That fleeting moment of holding the numbers in your mind captures the essence of working memory. At its core, working memory is the mental workspace where information is temporarily held and manipulated. It's the cognitive equivalent of a computer's RAM. It provides the necessary capacity to keep relevant information accessible for immediate use. This concept, introduced by cognitive psychologists Alan Baddeley and Graham Hitch in 1974, revolutionized our understanding of mental processes. It highlights how our minds do not merely store information but actively work with it.

Understanding working memory requires delving into its core components and the intricate dance they perform to facilitate our cognitive abilities. Imagine working memory as a mental stage where various performers (components) work together to produce seamless cognitive performances.

These performers can be broadly classified into three key players:

- verbal working memory
- visual working memory
- episodic buffer

Verbal working memory

Verbal working memory, similar to a mental recorder, handles auditory and linguistic information. Consider the experience of trying to remember someone's name while being introduced to several people at a party. This mental juggling act involves storing and rehearsing verbal information. It's crucial to temporarily hold spoken words in our minds and use mental repetition mechanisms to keep those words in our conscious awareness. This allows us to process and retain important information more effectively, facilitating better understanding and recall.

Visual working memory

Visual working memory, on the other hand, deals with visual and spatial information. Imagine navigating a new city using a map on your phone. Your visual working memory is at play as you glance at the map and look up to find the next street. It temporarily stores the visual information and helps you mentally visualize the map to make sense of your surroundings. This mental sketchpad allows you to manipulate and interact with visual and spatial data, making it essential for tasks ranging from reading and writing to complex problem-solving.

Episodic buffer

The episodic buffer acts as the integrative component of working memory, combining information from both verbal and visual systems and linking them to long-term memory. Imagine recalling where you parked your car in a large parking lot. The episodic buffer creates a cohesive mental representation by integrating the visual layout of the parking lot with verbal cues, such as section identifiers or remembered conversations about the parking spot.

Working memory is not just a passive storage system; it actively processes and manipulates information.

Time Blindness

Hindsight allows you to recall and visualize past events, informing your current decisions and actions. This ability to reflect on the past then connects to foresight, which involves anticipating and planning for future events based on that past information. If you have ADHD, impaired working memory disrupts this process, leading to difficulties in using hindsight and foresight effectively. Consequently, this disruption results in time blindness. The issue with hindsight impacts your ability to recall past events and understand their sequence and duration. This issue cascades to foresight and the estimation of future timeframes.

41

You might struggle to predict how long tasks will take and plan accordingly.

Working memory has its limitations by default. However, ADHD exacerbates them. Age, for instance, plays a significant role, with working memory typically peaking in young adulthood and gradually declining with age. Unfortunately, ADHD fosters the decline. You might notice that your working memory capacity is lower compared to neurotypical peers. For example, as a 35-year-old with ADHD, you may struggle with working memory tasks as much as a 60-year-old man without ADHD. At your job, diminished working memory can make it challenging to follow multi-step instructions, leading to frequent errors and the need for repeated guidance.

4. EMOTIONAL SELF-REGULATION

Ethan and Lily, his patient and loving partner, had built a life together. One evening, after a long day at work, Ethan came home to find the kitchen in disarray. Lily had accidentally spilled coffee on his favorite book.

His anger flared, and he yelled at her, calling her all sorts of names. Lily, hurt and shocked, retreated to the bedroom in tears. The following day, she packed her bags and left, unable to endure the cycle of hurt that persisted for years. Guilt gnawed at Ethan as he realized the damage caused by his outbursts, not to the book but to their relationship.

Emotional self-regulation is our ability to manage feelings healthily. It's not about hiding emotions but understanding and managing them effectively. Unfortunately, ADHD significantly impacts emotional self-regulation, leading to impulsive reactions and difficulty managing emotions (Barkley, 2015). However, ADHD doesn't amplify emotions any more than it does for neurotypical individuals. It's not like having "spider senses" that make you hyper-aware of every emotional nuance. People with ADHD experience emotions similarly to everyone else; the difference lies in the regulation of these emotions. Picture having a car with highly sensitive brakes and accelerator—minor emotional triggers can cause intense reactions. This doesn't mean you feel emotions more deeply, but your response might be more immediate and less filtered. The challenge is not in the intensity of emotions but in the speed and appropriateness of the response.

As we saw before, this difficulty in controlling responses is closely related to a lack of inhibition. ADHD impacts the brain's executive functions, which are responsible for self-control and regulation. It's as if your brain's filter is more porous, allowing impulsive reactions to slip through more easily. The result is a more erratic emotional response, not due to heightened sensitivity but because of reduced control over inhibitions. This means managing emotions can be more challenging, leading to reactions that might seem exaggerated or poorly timed, even though the underlying emotional experience is typical.

For individuals like Ethan, minor irritations can quickly escalate into intense outbursts. Friends and loved ones might forgive a lack of focus, forgetfulness, or frequent interruptions. However, they don't forgive the emotional damage you inflict. The pain and hurt caused by impulsive anger leave lasting scars. People remember how you made them feel, and emotional wounds are difficult to heal.

In Chapter 10, you'll discover effective strategies to manage your emotions and responses, particularly during communication with your partner.

5. SELF-MOTIVATION

"I have not failed. I've just found 10,000 ways that won't work."

Thomas Edison is widely considered one of the greatest inventors of all time. Edison's pursuit of the electric light bulb is a masterclass of perseverance. The road to his groundbreaking invention was anything but smooth. Edison's lab in Menlo Park became a crucible of experimentation, where he and his team worked tirelessly, often through the night. The lab was filled with the smell of burning filaments and the clatter of machinery. You could hear the constant hum of conversation as Edison and his team brainstormed solutions.

A series of failures marked Edison's journey—over a thousand unsuccessful attempts. Yet, his reaction to these failures was nothing short of extraordinary. Instead of seeing them as setbacks, Edison viewed each failure as a step closer to success. This mindset exemplifies the essence of self-motivation—the ability to stay focused and driven despite numerous obstacles.

Edison's story is not just about persistence but about an inner drive that transformed setbacks into stepping stones. It demonstrates a crucial mindset for any aspiring leader.

The power of self-motivation is an essential ingredient in the recipe for success. It transforms ordinary individuals into extraordinary achievers. It fuels the energy of leaders and inspires admiration and respect from peers. How could they get better results from such an abstract concept? It may not be that abstract. It goes deep inside your bones, or better, your brain. The physiological underpinnings of motivation provide a scientific basis for understanding it. While cars can rely on different types of fuel to run, such as gasoline, diesel, electric batteries, and hydrogen, your motivation can count only on one. Dopamine, often referred to as the "feel-good" neurotransmitter, plays a crucial role in your brain. It works on your motivation and reward pathways. In particular, achieving set goals raises dopamine levels, reinforcing successful behaviors. Understanding this biological mechanism can help you harness your leadership.

Stay confident. In Chapter 5, we'll explore the science of ADHD and the solutions that can immediately bring out the hero in you.

6. PLANNING AND PROBLEM-SOLVING

"The purpose of thinking is to let the ideas die instead of us dying." — Alfred North Whitehead.

Whitehead's quote highlights the essential nature of thinking, where ideas are tested, refined, and discarded as needed to ensure our survival. This process allows us to evaluate potential actions and outcomes without needing to experience them directly. For instance, through thinking and understanding, you can predict the consequences of jumping from a cliff. Therefore, you don't need to leap off to discover the fatal result. This capacity to foresee and avoid danger through thought alone underscores the critical role of intellectual processes in our ability to navigate and thrive in the world.

This principle is at the heart of planning and problem-solving. By evaluating your ideas, you prevent potential failures and setbacks from harming you. Effective planning and problem-solving allow you to address challenges preemptively, turning potential threats into opportunities for growth and success.

If you have ADHD, your ability to plan is often weakened. We've talked about working memory before—the mental workspace where you compare past experiences with current situations to make better decisions. ADHD makes it harder to hold onto and use this information, which means you might struggle to remember what worked or didn't in the past, making it harder to plan for the future. Furthermore, problem-solving is also impacted. Maintaining motivation when faced with frustrating tasks is crucial to support goal-directed behavior. However, due to self-regulation issues, when frustration sets in, it can sap motivation. This makes it hard to initiate or persist with problem-solving efforts.

EXECUTIVE FUNCTIONS IMPACT

Now that you have a clear grasp of EF, here's a recap on how ADHD disrupts performance.

Firstly, the inability to plan the future jeopardizes long-term objectives. If you can't develop compelling long-term goals, delaying gratification becomes a significant challenge.

Secondly, distractions easily divert attention, steering you off-course. Here, inhibition is insufficient. Any passing distraction can captivate your focus, pulling you away from your goals. Emotional inhibition also plays a crucial role. Without it, minor setbacks can spiral into intense emotions and disruptive thoughts. This emotional turbulence makes problem-solving and persistence particularly challenging.

Lastly, returning to the original task becomes extremely challenging after you have been distracted. Bad working memory is to blame again since it makes it difficult to remember and resume previously interrupted tasks. That exacerbates further a cycle of inefficiency and frustration.

Despite the challenges associated with EFs and their impact on success, there is a profound reason to remain hopeful. Advances in neuroscience and psychology have revealed how to develop and strengthen EFs, and cutting-edge research is identifying specific interventions that can enhance these skills.

Take your time to understand the next chapter. It's a bit complex but very important.

TAKEAWAYS

1. **Nature of ADHD:** ADHD is fundamentally a problem of self-regulation, affecting the ability to control impulses and behaviors effectively.

2. **Impact on Brain Functions:** It significantly affects brain areas related to executive functions, impairing task and activity management.

3. **Effect on Self-Awareness:** ADHD disrupts self-awareness, making it challenging to assess one's own behaviors and actions accurately.

4. **Inhibition Challenges:** It causes difficulties in controlling impulsive actions and reactions.

5. **Working Memory Deficits:** It hinders the ability to hold and manipulate information over short periods.

6. **Emotional Self-Regulation:** ADHD affects emotional self-regulation, leading to challenges in appropriately managing and responding to emotions.

7. **Challenges in Self-Motivation:** It impacts self-motivation, making it harder to initiate and sustain task effort.

8. **Planning and Problem Solving:** It hinders planning and problem-solving abilities, complicating organizing and executing tasks efficiently.

PART 2

Brain-Boosting Solutions for ADHD

Chapter 5: Balancing Brain Networks and Boosting Focus

August 13, 1876. The date of the inaugural performance of Richard Wagner's monumental "Der Ring des Nibelungen" at the Bayreuth Festival. It was not just an opera but a grand spectacle that redefined the very essence of musical drama. The epic tetralogy required an impressive 120-piece orchestra. The scale of the orchestra created an awe-inspiring experience that left audiences breathless. This monumental achievement was only possible because of Wagner. Without his rhythm, the 120 world-class musicians would leave the audience in chaos and disappointment.

Similarly, the brain has many circuits. They interact with each other under the guidance of a brain area that maintains the rhythm. But what happens when the brain's Conductor does not show up?

THE SCIENCE BEHIND DISTRACTION IN ADHD

The interaction between the default mode network (DMN) and task-positive networks (TPN) is crucial for brain functioning.

The DMN is active when you are not focusing on the outside world. It's like your brain's "idle mode." When you're daydreaming, thinking about yourself, or recalling memories. It involves reflective activities and helps you process emotions, imagine scenarios, and reflect on your experiences. Instead, the TPN is crucial when you engage in goal-oriented activities. This network is active when you focus on tasks that need attention, such as preparing a presentation or participating in a meeting.

In individuals without ADHD, these networks are anti-correlated; when the DMN is active, the TPN is not, and vice versa. This anti-correlation is crucial for efficient cognitive functioning and it allows you to switch smoothly between rest and goal-directed activities.

However, if you have ADHD, this relationship is disrupted. The DMN and TPN tend to be more synchronized, leading to an overlap in their activity, which can cause significant attentional issues.

But who is the conductor of the Orchestra? And why does it not coordinate the DMN and TPN efficiently?

The prefrontal cortex (PFC), located just behind the forehead, is the conductor. The PFC is the critical part of the brain for suppressing irrelevant information and enhancing focus on relevant tasks.

When individuals without ADHD focus on external tasks, the PFC suppresses the DMN (default mode network). However, if you have ADHD, this suppression is often inadequate. Therefore, it leads to persistent internal chatter and difficulty maintaining focus. Think about trying to read a book while a TV is playing in the background—your attention keeps getting pulled away, making it hard to concentrate.

Many studies found a significant inefficiency in PFC functioning. In particular, Bush, Valera, and Seidman (2005) analyzed over 50 neuroimaging studies and concluded that the PFC showed a 25% reduction in activity in individuals with ADHD. In addition, two more key players exacerbate the issues of distraction and lack of focus.

DOPAMINE AND NOREPINEPHRINE

Dopamine is a chemical in the brain that plays a key role in reward, motivation, and pleasure. This neuromodulator supports sustained attention by acting like the brain's noise-canceling headphones. It helps the prefrontal cortex filter out irrelevant stimuli, enhancing focus on relevant tasks. Unfortunately, when you have ADHD, dopamine levels are lower, leaving you unprotected from extraneous thoughts or sensory inputs. In particular, Volkow et al. (2009) found that those with ADHD had a 15-20% reduction in dopamine receptor availability.

Norepinephrine, another critical neuromodulator, has a different priority. It acts primarily to amplify signals that are deemed relevant, thereby increasing alertness and focus. Norepinephrine enhances the PFC's ability to prioritize and sustain attention on specific tasks. Arnsten (2009) emphasized the importance of dopamine and norepinephrine in regulating PFC function. Conducted at Yale University, Arnsten's research showed that even a slight decrease in norepinephrine levels led to a 40% reduction in PFC-mediated tasks.

Dopamine and norepinephrine work together to create a balanced environment by reducing unnecessary background noise and amplifying significant stimuli. Such collaboration leads to improved focus and attention. In individuals with ADHD, the dysregulation of these neuromodulators results in the characteristic difficulties with maintaining attention, controlling impulses, and managing hyperactivity.

Then how can we boost those neurotransmitters, activate the prefrontal cortex, and get rid of ADHD?

TAKEAWAYS

1. **Network Interference:** In ADHD, the Default Mode Network (DMN) and Task Positive Network (TPN) work simultaneously, leading to low focus and poor inhibition.

2. **Prefrontal Cortex:** The Prefrontal Cortex (PFC) is not efficiently active in coordinating these two networks.

3. **Neurotransmitter Deficiency:** Norepinephrine and dopamine levels are low in ADHD, further affecting attention and executive function.

Chapter 6: Medications and Their Effect on Brain Function

In the bustling city of New York during the late 1930s, a young boy named Tommy struggles to fit in at school. Tommy was bright and curious, but his inability to sit still and focus during lessons led to frequent reprimands from his teachers. Due to his impulsiveness, he couldn't make friends, leaving him feeling misunderstood and isolated. Tommy's parents, extremely frustrated, became determined to find a solution. They took him to Dr. Charles Bradley, a pioneering psychiatrist at the Emma Pendleton Bradley Home, a center specializing in children with behavioral issues. Dr. Bradley had recently started experimenting with a new stimulant medication called Benzedrine. While initially used to treat conditions like nasal congestion, Dr. Bradley had observed that the medication seemed to have a calming effect on some children with behavioral issues. With his parents' consent, Tommy began taking Benzedrine under Dr. Bradley's supervision. To everyone's amazement, Tommy's change was almost immediate. His teachers noticed he could sit through an entire lesson, he began to complete his assignments, and his grades improved. For the first time, Tommy felt he could keep up with his peers, and he started to enjoy school.

Tommy's transformation marked a new era in treating hyperactivity and attention disorders.

By the 1950s, ADHD treatment advanced significantly with the introduction of methylphenidate, known as Ritalin. This new medication offered an alternative to Benzedrine and quickly became a cornerstone in managing ADHD. Families nationwide found hope in Ritalin, as it helped children like Tommy focus better on their education and engage meaningfully with their peers. Since then, medications have been widely used to improve ADHD, and understanding the different types is crucial in managing ADHD effectively. These medications fall into two categories: stimulants and non-stimulants.

Stimulants, including well-known names like Adderall, Ritalin, and Vyvanse, have long been the go-to solution for treating ADHD. Their popularity stems from their remarkable ability to boost focus and curb impulsive behavior, making them a reliable choice for many.

For those who might not find stimulants suitable for them, non-stimulants offer a valuable alternative. Medications like Strattera (atomoxetine) and Intuniv (guanfacine) work differently from stimulants. Yet, they also can effectively manage ADHD symptoms, providing a broader range of options.

Let's explore how those medications have been helping millions suffering from ADHD.

STIMULANT MEDICATIONS

To calm a storm, add more wind. It sounds counterintuitive. Yet, this is the intriguing paradox of using stimulants to manage ADHD, a condition often marked by hyperactivity. How can drugs that ramp up the nervous system help those who are already bouncing off the walls?

The answer lies in a deeper understanding of ADHD. As explained in Chapter 3, the primary challenge isn't just hyperactivity; it's impulsivity and an inability to maintain focus. Stimulants help by fine-tuning the brain's capacity to regulate attention and behavior. They act like the conductor, orchestrating neural circuits to harmonize focus and impulse control, transforming chaos into a concerted effort.

Ritalin

Ritalin was one of the earliest medications used for ADHD, as doctors commonly prescribed it in the 1990s. Ritalin (methylphenidate) primarily increases dopamine levels in the brain by blocking reabsorption (Volkow et al., 2005). This mechanism helps improve focus and attention by enhancing the brain's signal-to-noise ratio, making it easier to discard irrelevant stimuli.

However, Ritalin lost some market share to Adderall. Many consider this stimulant more efficient since it applies three powerful mechanisms (Faraone, 2018).

Adderall

Picture the brain's neurotransmitter system as a supply chain. Dopamine and norepinephrine are valuable products to deliver so that the city's economy (brain functions) runs smoothly. Let's use bottled water as an example of the product (neurotransmitters).

- Neurotransmitters: Think of them as essential products like bottled water, with dopamine and norepinephrine as prime examples.

- Synaptic Cleft: This is the space between neurons where neurotransmitters' exchange occurs, akin to a store where customers purchase water.

- Presynaptic Neurons: Picture them as suppliers or warehouses, storing and releasing neurotransmitters.

- Postsynaptic Neurons: These are the customers buying bottled water.

The presynaptic neuron (warehouse) releases neurotransmitters (bottled water) into the synaptic cleft (stores). They then travel across this space to bind to receptors on the postsynaptic neuron (customers), where they exert their effects.

Here are the three mechanisms Adderall uses to improve transportation efficiency and availability:

First, it inhibits the reabsorption of neurotransmitters by presynaptic transporters. Without Adderall, these presynaptic transporters (suppliers) would quickly reabsorb the dopamine and norepinephrine, reducing their availability in the synaptic cleft (stores). However, things change when we add Adderall. Picture a policy change where stores can no longer return unsold bottled water to the warehouses. As a result, more bottled water remains on store shelves (synaptic cleft), making it readily available for customers (postsynaptic receptors).

Next, we look at the disruption of Vesicular Monoamine Transporter 2 (VMAT2).

VMAT2 is a protein involved in the transport of neurotransmitters. Without Adderall, the VMAT2 packages neurotransmitters into vesicles, resulting in less frequent release into the synaptic cleft. Things change once you add Adderall. Imagine that the warehouse bypasses the process of packaging bottled water into boxes of six. Shipping becomes faster because the warehouse loads individual bottles onto the delivery trucks. This increases the amount of bottled water (neurotransmitters) ready for delivery, ensuring higher availability in the synapse (stores).

Finally, consider the increased release of neurotransmitters. Without Adderall, the release of neurotransmitters would be more controlled and less frequent. However, with Adderall, things change. Suppose that the company decides to double the fleet of delivery trucks. Now, the stores receive water more frequently throughout the day. This mechanism ensures that stores (synapses) are consistently stocked with bottled water (neurotransmitters).

Putting it all together, here's how Adderall works:

- It stops the collection trucks from returning bottled water to the warehouse.
- It bypassed the packaging process to make bottled water immediately available.
- It increases the number of delivery trucks on the road.

Those three mechanisms help the stores (synaptic cleft) stay well-stocked, ensuring that customers (postsynaptic receptors) always have access to the water they need (dopamine and norepinephrine). Such mechanisms keep the city's economy (brain functions) running efficiently.

Vyvanse

Vyvanse (lisdexamfetamine) is a prodrug, which means it is inactive until metabolized. There, it converts into dextroamphetamine. This conversion process makes Vyvanse a time-release stimulant, which helps maintain stable levels in the bloodstream (Goodman, 2010).

Vyvanse and Adderall differ notably in their release mechanisms and duration of action, impacting how they fit into daily routines. Vyvanse features a time-release mechanism that lasts 12 to 14 hours, providing all-day coverage but risking overstimulation late into the evening, which can interfere with sleep. Adderall, on the other hand, offers both immediate-release (IR) and extended-release (XR) forms. The IR form works quickly, making it ideal for immediate symptom relief, but it only lasts 4-6 hours, requiring multiple doses throughout the day. This can lead to periods where symptoms are not well-controlled and may cause a rebound effect, where symptoms return more intensely once the medication wears off. The XR form uses a dual-bead delivery system to immediately release half of the dose and the other half gradually, providing effects for up to 12 hours. This offers extended relief with fewer doses but poses a risk of late-day stimulation, similar to Vyvanse.

Why Are We Giving Meth to People?

This provocative question echoes a common fear: Are we handing out drugs like methamphetamine to adults and kids? It's a concern that strikes at the heart of parental anxiety. However, the truth is far more nuanced and reassuring.

While it's true that medications like Adderall contain amphetamines, equating them with street drugs oversimplifies their purpose and safety. The pharmacological profiles and effects of prescription stimulants differ significantly from those of illicit substances. Strict medical supervision aims to formulate precise and controlled dosages of these medications. This regulation drastically reduces the risk of abuse and the severe side effects that are hallmarks of street drug use. Even something as benign as water can be deadly if consumed excessively. Similarly, while amphetamines in medications like Adderall can be beneficial when used correctly, misuse leads to severe consequences.

NON-STIMULANTS: ALTERNATIVES AND COMPLEMENTS

While stimulants are often celebrated for their efficacy in managing symptoms of ADHD, they are not suitable for everyone. Unfortunately, they can lead to a range of side effects, including:

- Insomnia

- Appetite Suppression

- Jitteriness and Anxiety

- Increased Heart Rate and Blood Pressure

For those who experience adverse effects or have contraindications, non-stimulant medications offer a promising alternative. Two of the most notable non-stimulant medications are Strattera (atomoxetine) and Intuniv (guanfacine). These medications not only provide a valuable option for those who cannot tolerate stimulants but also serve as effective complements in certain treatment plans.

Strattera

Strattera is a selective norepinephrine reuptake inhibitor (NRI) that increases norepinephrine levels. Remember the supply chain example? Think of the policy change where stores can no longer return unsold bottled water to the warehouses. As a result, more bottled water remains on store shelves (synaptic cleft), making it readily available for customers (postsynaptic receptors). However, the policy only applies to sparkling water (norepinephrine) but not to still water (dopamine).

This mechanism can be particularly beneficial for individuals who do not respond well to stimulants. Numerous studies, including a pivotal trial by Michelson et al. (2002), showed Strattera's efficacy in improving attention and impulsive behaviors.

Intuniv (guanfacine)

Professionals often use Intuniv as an adjunct to stimulant medications, providing support for individuals with complex symptom profiles. Intuniv works by activating alpha-2A adrenergic receptors in the prefrontal cortex, enhancing its ability to regulate attention, behavior, and emotions. This action strengthens the activity of the prefrontal cortex, crucial for executive functions (Arnsten, 2011). Unlike stimulants, Intuniv does not increase the amount of norepinephrine. Instead, it makes the brain more sensitive to the norepinephrine already present, allowing for more efficient cognitive processing, much like a well-organized store where customers can easily find and use products.

Trial And Error

Medications have been an important aid in overcoming ADHD. However, the journey to finding the accurate ADHD medication is often one of trial and error. Each individual's response varies based on genetic factors, the nature of symptoms, and overall health profile. Unfortunately, research indicates that about 50% of adults discontinue their medication within the first year, often due to side effects or lack of perceived efficacy (Adler et al., 2009). This highlights the necessity for personalized treatment plans and regular follow-ups to adjust dosages and address concerns.

The risk related to the wrong dosage of medication is often underrated, so much so that even individuals without ADHD indulge in those powerful substances.

Many individuals misuse stimulants like Adderall to boost focus and productivity, but the consequences can be dangerous. For those with ADHD, these medications help balance dopamine levels, improving concentration and impulse control. However, without ADHD and medical guidance, these drugs can disrupt the brain's natural chemistry, leading to harmful side effects. The non-prescription use of Adderall and other stimulants is alarmingly prevalent, especially among students and professionals. Driven by relentless academic and professional pressures, many young adults turn to these drugs to enhance focus and productivity. Surveys reveal that up to 25% of college students and 35% of individuals aged 17 to 30 regularly use Adderall for studying or working despite not having an ADHD diagnosis (Center on Addiction, 2019). This trend underscores a significant shift in how these substances are perceived and utilized. Stimulants like Adderall have become almost as ubiquitous as caffeine in the quest for a cognitive edge.

The misuse of these substances leads to problems beyond addiction. Artificial dopamine floods disrupt the brain's delicate chemistry, increasing the risk of severe side effects such as anxiety, paranoia, and psychosis.

Furthermore, the use of medication for ADHD presents a multifaceted challenge. Central to this issue is the inherent risk of human error in diagnosing the disorder. ADHD frequently coexists with other disorders that can obscure the primary cause of symptoms and lead to inappropriate medication choices.

In the next chapter, you will learn the intricate web of disorders that overlap with ADHD, emphasizing the critical need for careful differentiation. Only by acknowledging and understanding the interplay between ADHD and these co-occurring conditions can you avoid the immense risks associated with misdiagnosis and mistreatment, paving the way for more accurate and effective solutions.

TAKEAWAYS

1. **Stimulant Medications:** Stimulants like Ritalin, Adderall, and Vyvanse are widely used for ADHD treatment, helping to improve focus and reduce impulsivity.

2. **Non-Stimulant Medications:** Non-stimulants such as Intuniv and Strattera are also used for ADHD, offering alternative treatment options.

3. **Mechanism of Action:** Medications work on dopamine and norepinephrine, key neurotransmitters involved in attention and behavior regulation.

Chapter 7: The Importance of Comorbidities in Accurate Diagnoses

Richard Fee, a promising young man from Virginia Beach, had a bright future. As a high school valedictorian and college scholarship recipient, he aspired to become a medical professional. However, his life took a tragic turn. Fee's troubles began in college when he was first prescribed Adderall to help manage his studies. What started as a tool for academic success quickly spiraled into dependence. He began misusing the drug, seeking higher doses, and falsifying symptoms to obtain more prescriptions. His addiction grew, leading to severe mood swings, paranoia, and insomnia.

Fee's family, alarmed by his deteriorating mental state, tried to intervene multiple times. Unfortunately, the ease with which Fee could obtain his medication thwarted their efforts. The healthcare system failed to provide the necessary safeguards. Despite numerous red flags and desperate pleas from his parents, Richard continued to receive prescriptions. His escalating dependence on Adderall eventually led to his tragic demise. At just 25 years old, Fee was found dead in his apartment, a victim of the very medication meant to aid him.

In the wake of Richard Fee's tragic death, his family channeled their grief into action, founding the Richard Fee Foundation. This nonprofit organization aims to raise awareness about the dangers of prescription drug misuse and advocate for better mental health support. Their mission is to prevent other families from enduring similar heartache. One cornerstone initiative of the foundation is its educational outreach, explaining the importance of making accurate diagnoses. Various disorders can significantly impact executive functioning (EF), often leading to misdiagnoses. Understanding these risks helps us better identify and differentiate between conditions.

Disorders such as autism spectrum disorder, bipolar disorder, anxiety, and depression impair these executive functions, and recognizing these overlaps with ADHD is crucial for accurate diagnosis and effective treatment.

AUTISM

Autism Spectrum Disorder (ASD) is a complex neurodevelopmental condition characterized by persistent challenges in social interaction, communication, and behavior. Around 40-60% of those diagnosed with ASD also exhibit symptoms of ADHD (Duke Autism Center). This intersection is not merely coincidental; it stems from the shared impact of both disorders on executive function (EF) (Kenworthy et al., 2008).

Individuals with ASD often face challenges with language and social interaction. Such challenges impact their verbal working memory, which makes it harder to hold and manipulate verbal information (Hill, 2004). Consequently, ASD affects crucial cognitive abilities and hinders the development of skills like planning and problem-solving (Kenworthy et al., 2008). As we saw previously, these EF challenges are common in ADHD, highlighting the overlap between the two conditions.

The relationship between ASD and ADHD is complex and multifaceted. While their symptoms overlap, the underlying causes of EF deficits differ. In ASD, EF impairments relate to overall brain development, with social and communicative challenges playing a crucial role. In ADHD, EF deficits are more directly related to prefrontal cortex dysfunction, affecting attentional control and impulsivity, independent of social and communicative factors (Hill, 2004).

Stimulants like Adderall can worsen ASD challenges as they can increase anxiety, repetitive behaviors, irritability, and mood swings (Psychology Today, 2020).

DEPRESSION

Depression can disguise itself as ADHD, and the similarities between these conditions can be misleading (Bron, Bijlenga, Verduijn et al., 2016). For example, rumination—a key feature of depression where individuals dwell on negative thoughts—diverts mental resources and further hampers executive functioning (Watkins & Brown, 2002; Fossati, Ergis, & Allilaire, 2002). Despite these overlaps, it is crucial to recognize that not everyone with depression has ADHD. The main difference lies in the chronic nature and underlying causes. Marked by persistent issues in self-regulation, ADHD is a neurodevelopmental disorder as the symptoms and challenges are often present in childhood. In contrast, depressive episodes can occur at any stage of life, triggered by a mix of genetic, environmental, and psychological factors.

Using stimulants prescribed for ADHD can pose significant risks for individuals with depression since these medications can worsen anxiety, agitation, and insomnia. Additionally, the side effects of stimulants, such as increased heart rate and blood pressure, may pose further health risks (Smith, 2022). Again, accurate diagnosis and tailored treatment are essential to avoid more harm than good.

BIPOLAR DISORDER

Bipolar disorder adds another layer of complexity to diagnosing mental health conditions. During manic episodes, individuals may display impulsivity and restlessness, closely resembling ADHD symptoms. However, these bipolar manifestations are episodic, fluctuating dramatically with mood cycles. In contrast, ADHD's executive function deficits are chronic and pervasive, as they typically originate in childhood and persist over time. While understanding the distinction between these conditions is crucial for effective treatment, the diagnosis can be complicated. Imagine that approximately 20% of adults with ADHD also have bipolar disorder (ADDitude, Rodden, & Olivardia, 2024).

The risk of misdiagnosis becomes even more pronounced regarding medication management. Stimulants can have dangerous repercussions for individuals with bipolar disorder as stimulants can lead to increased mood instability, heightened impulsivity, and even psychosis (ADDitude, Rodden, & Olivardia, 2024).

Mental health professionals must carefully assess the patient's history, symptom patterns, and mood fluctuations to differentiate between these overlapping conditions. Failure to do so can result in treatment plans that worsen the patient's overall mental health.

The challenge of making an accurate diagnosis is significant. If you are hesitant to consider medication, remember that alternative options are available. In the next chapter, you'll learn alternative ways to manage ADHD effectively. In particular, you'll discover what other tools can increase dopamine and norepinephrine levels to enhance PFC activation.

TAKEAWAYS

1. **Risk of Misdiagnosis:** ADHD often overlaps with other disorders, increasing the risk of misdiagnosis.

2. **Medication Effects:** Medications used for ADHD can lead to negative effects if used for other disorders.

3. **Guidance:** The process of finding the right medication for ADHD involves trial and error and requires careful medical guidance.

Chapter 8: Effective Non-Medication Solutions to Improve Focus

The circadian rhythm, a fundamental biological cycle inherent in all living beings, dictates the patterns of daily existence—from sleeping and waking to metabolic functions. Imagine this rhythm as a steady, reliable current in a river, carrying you effortlessly through day and night. Adhering to this natural schedule allows your body to function optimally, like a boat smoothly navigating with the flow. However, when you resist—staying awake against your body's signals or waking up too early—you start swimming against a formidable current. Each movement becomes strenuous, your energy depletes faster, and you feel drained.

Based on that, we'll examine factors like sleep, light, nutrition, and exercise to positively impact your circadian rhythm and the sleep-wake cycle, leading to better regulation of neurotransmitters like dopamine and norepinephrine.

By the end of this chapter, you will be able to apply practical strategies to increase PFC activation and effectiveness.

SLEEP

Would you work all day for free? That's what happens to your brain when you don't sleep well. Sleep is a crucial pillar of your overall well-being, and its importance extends beyond mere rest. Inadequate sleep can severely impair executive functions. For example, during deep non-REM sleep, your brain processes and consolidates information from the day, transferring it from short-term to long-term memory (Diekelmann & Born, 2010).

Moreover, sleep deprivation can undermine your ability to focus and maintain attention. When you are well-rested, your prefrontal cortex (PFC) operates efficiently. However, poor sleep reduces PFC activity, which impacts concentration, decision-making, and impulse control (Tai, Chen, Manohar, & Husain, 2022). Additionally, the amygdala, responsible for processing emotions, becomes more reactive when sleep-deprived (van der Helm, Gujar, & Walker, 2010). This heightened reactivity can lead to increased stress, anxiety, and mood swings, making it harder to manage your feelings.

Unfortunately, if you have ADHD, you are 50% to 75% more likely to experience sleep problems. However, don't despair, as there are plenty of tools that exist to improve this statistic (Bijlenga, Vollebregt, Kooij, & Arns, 2019).

First, establishing a consistent wake-up and sleep time is essential. Your body thrives on routine, and sticking to a regular sleep schedule helps regulate your internal clock. Think of your sleep schedule like the gears of a well-oiled machine. When the gears are in sync, the machine runs smoothly and efficiently. Similarly, a regular sleep schedule creates a seamless flow in your daily life, leading to more restful nights and energized days. Start by setting a wake-up time that you can consistently follow most days. Then, calculate 7-9 hours of sleep and define your bedtime. This is the first habit to set yourself up for mental and physical success.

Sleep Environment

Creating a sleep-friendly environment is essential. Picture your bedroom as a sanctuary for rest, where noise, heat, and light wait outside. While sleeping with an eye mask and earplugs is far from sexy, your partner will appreciate your mood in the morning. Also, try to set the room temperature to a cool and comfortable level. These adjustments create a cocoon-like atmosphere, paving the way for deep, uninterrupted sleep.

Besides these physical adjustments, incorporating relaxation techniques into your nightly routine improves sleep quality. Breathing exercises, for instance, can calm your mind and body, preparing you for a peaceful night. Imagine slowly inhaling the crisp air of a serene forest, filling your lungs with calmness and exhaling stress and tension. Similarly, when you take a warm bath before bed, your muscles relax, and your body tells you it's time to sleep. If nothing works, try progressive muscle relaxation. This technique involves tensing and releasing different muscle groups, alleviating tension, and promoting sleep.

Apply these practices in your daily routine and notice how this transforms your sleep experience and, consequently, your quality of life. Let's now examine the three variables you can tweak to enhance sleep and executive functions.

1. LIGHT

Your evening routine starts in the morning. Morning light exposure significantly influences your crucial hormones, including melatonin and cortisol. Melatonin, which promotes sleep, lowers in the morning light (Zeitzer et al., 2000). This ensures melatonin levels rise later, promoting sleepiness around 14-16 hours after waking. Cortisol is essential for bodily functions like regulating metabolism and controlling the sleep-wake cycle. Morning light helps synchronize cortisol levels, which peak in the early morning, providing alertness for the day (Petrowski et al., 2020). Therefore, one of the best ways to start your day is by getting bright sunlight within 30 to 60 minutes of waking (Huberman, 2023).

This practice isn't just about soaking up rays. Sunlight hitting your eyes stimulates your internal clock and signals that it's time to be active. Throughout the day, sun exposure remains essential. Getting outside around sunset sends vital signals to your brain, indicating that nighttime is approaching (Huberman, 2023). This adjusts your internal clock, making it easier to transition into a restful state as the evening progresses; it's a way to balance daytime stimulation with nighttime preparation.

Finally, after sunset, create an environment that aligns with the natural decrease in light. Bright artificial lights can interfere with this process, confusing your internal clocks and making it harder to fall asleep. To counteract this, dim the lights as soon as evening falls. Use desk lamps instead of harsh overhead lights, and opt for the soft glow of candlelight. This gentle lighting mimics the natural light progression of the day, helping your body recognize it's time to relax and prepare for rest.

2. NUTRITION AND SUPPLEMENTS

Diet plays a crucial role in the manifestation and management of ADHD symptoms, and changes can lead to remarkable behavior and mental function improvements.

Eliminating simple sugars is the most universally recommended dietary change for managing ADHD. While sugar doesn't directly cause ADHD, it can influence the severity of symptoms. Fluctuations in blood sugar levels can lead to headaches, drowsiness, and irritability. While lowering sugar intake doesn't cure ADHD, it might help reduce the reliance on medication. In particular, many report improved concentration, reduced impulsivity, and better emotional regulation (Johnson et al. 2011).

If you have ADHD you might also consider the oligoantigenic diet which aims at identifying and eliminating foods that cause mild allergies or sensitivities. Research shows that even mild food sensitivities can worsen ADHD symptoms and removing these allergens will likely improve mood and concentration (Pelsser et al., 2011).

Caffeine

Centuries ago, a young goat herder named Kaldi roamed the hills of Ethiopia, tending to his flock. One fateful day, he noticed his goats behaving exuberantly, almost dancing on their hind legs, bleating, and prancing with unusual energy. Intrigued, Kaldi observed that the goats had been nibbling on the bright red berries of a nearby shrub. Driven by curiosity, Kaldi plucked a handful of these mysterious berries and tasted them himself. To his astonishment, he felt a surge of energy and alertness. Eager to share his discovery, Kaldi gathered some of the berries and hurried to the local monastery. The monks, initially skeptical, decided to experiment with the berries. They threw them into the fire, releasing a tantalizing aroma that filled the air. The roasted beans were then crushed, mixed with water, and consumed. This discovery revealed a drink that helped them stay awake during long hours of prayer and meditation. They loved it. They called it coffee.

Caffeine is still widely recognized for its role in boosting energy and alertness. It increases dopamine levels and the number of dopamine receptors in the brain. Think of dopamine receptors as "docking stations" for dopamine. The more docking stations you have, the better your brain can use dopamine, enhancing its positive effects on mood and motivation. In simple terms, caffeine helps your brain become more efficient at using dopamine.

However, it can also exacerbate the issue if not managed properly, leading to increased anxiety, jitteriness, and disrupted sleep patterns (Nehlig, 1999). Only a few know how to get the most out of it and enhance executive functions, relieving the struggles of ADHD.

Upon waking, the body is already clearing adenosine, a neurotransmitter that promotes sleep (Landolt, 2008). This natural process allows for a smoother transition from sleep to wakefulness, but if you interfere with this process in the morning, you'll face the consequences in the afternoon. Instead, by waiting to consume caffeine, you'll experience more stable energy for the rest of the day. Delay caffeine intake for 90 to 120 minutes after waking and say goodbye to the dreaded afternoon slump. Therefore, don't reach for a cup of coffee first thing in the morning.

It's also crucial to consider when to stop consuming caffeine since late consumption disrupts sleep. Consuming caffeine within 8-10 hours of bedtime can hinder sleep quality. This is because caffeine blocks adenosine receptors, delaying sleepiness and prolonging wakefulness. Enjoy your last caffeine intake in the early afternoon to maintain high motivation and alertness without sacrificing sleep (Landolt, 2008).

"I can't work without coffee." "Late caffeine doesn't affect my sleep." You might have spoken those words a few times, excusing your need for a fresh cup in the afternoon. However, caffeine can significantly impact your deep sleep stages without you noticing. Deep sleep is crucial for physical recovery and memory consolidation since it restores norepinephrine and dopamine levels. Missing this vital opportunity leads to cumulative sleep debt, and you might experience chronic fatigue, impaired cognitive function, and mood disturbances. Therefore, try shifting your caffeine consumption to earlier in the day; enjoy your coffee in the morning and a small cup right after lunch if you need it. This way, you can still get the boost you need without sacrificing sleep quality. Your body and mind will thank you!

Omega 3

In the complex landscape of essential nutrients for optimal brain health, Omega-3 fatty acids stand out. Omega-3 fatty acids, mainly found in fish oils, offer many health benefits, including anti-inflammatory properties. One of the key components of Omega-3 fatty acids is eicosapentaenoic acid (EPA). Recent research emphasizes EPA's crucial role in cognitive function and managing ADHD, and emerging studies suggest that a daily intake of 1000 milligrams of EPA improves cognitive performance in adults with ADHD. EPA's potential lies in its ability to enhance neurotransmitter function, support brain cell membrane health, and reduce brain inflammation. These effects collectively improve attention, reduce impulsivity, and enhance executive functioning (Hawkey & Nigg, 2019).

Melatonin

Remember those nights when you were lying in bed, the day's weight pressing down on you, but sleep remained elusive? I bet you would give anything for a magical solution that would send you peacefully into sleep. This nightly metamorphosis, orchestrated by a tiny gland in the brain, is vital to our well-being. The pineal gland produces a hormone that many have turned to for better sleep: melatonin. But as with many things in life, the story of melatonin is one of complexity, both in its promise and perils.

Melatonin supplements can be incredibly beneficial by regulating the sleep-wake cycle. Studies have shown that taking melatonin can decrease the time it takes to fall asleep, enhance sleep quality, and improve morning alertness (Ferracioli-Oda et al., 2013). It offers a glimmer of hope in the dark. However, this is just half of the story. While melatonin can be a helpful aid for short-term use, prolonged reliance on this supplement comes with concerns. One of the key issues lies in the hormonal balance it affects. The production of melatonin in the body is a finely tuned process influenced by the natural light-dark cycle. Introducing external sources of melatonin over long periods can disrupt this delicate balance, making it harder to maintain a consistent sleep pattern without supplements (Seabra et al., 2000).

Furthermore, research has highlighted inconsistencies in the amount of melatonin found in supplements. A study published in the Journal of Clinical Sleep Medicine found that the melatonin content in over-the-counter supplements often varies drastically from the labeled amount. Some products contained as little as 83% to over 478% of the labeled dose, posing risks to consumers. These discrepancies can lead to unintended side effects, such as daytime drowsiness, dizziness, headaches, and hormonal imbalances (Erland & Saxena, 2017).

Tips for Safe and Effective Use

Given the benefits and risks associated with melatonin, how can you navigate its use effectively? Here are some tips to help you make informed decisions:

- Consult a Healthcare Professional: Before starting melatonin, discuss it with your healthcare provider.

- Start with a Low Dose: The lowest effective dose is typically around 0.5 to 1 milligram. Higher doses are not necessarily more effective and can increase the risk of side effects. To avoid taking an incorrect amount, consider starting with an even smaller dose, such as 0.1 milligrams.

- Use Short-Term: Melatonin is best for short-term sleep issues, like adjusting to a new time zone or overcoming temporary insomnia. Avoid using it as a long-term solution unless advised by your healthcare provider.

- Monitor for Side Effects: Be aware of potential side effects such as headaches, dizziness, and digestive issues. If you experience any adverse effects, discontinue use and consult your healthcare professional.

Like many tools in our health arsenal, melatonin requires careful consideration and respect. It offers hope for those struggling with sleep but demands a mindful approach to avoid misuse. By understanding its benefits and risks, you can harness the power of melatonin to achieve restful nights and productive days.

3. EXERCISE

Imagine waking up to the gentle glow of dawn, the world still quiet and serene. You lace up your sneakers and take a deep breath of the crisp morning air. Exercising within the first three hours of waking is a secret weapon for boosting your brain and body.

Morning exercise is a powerful catalyst, triggering chemicals that enhance productivity and mood. Studies reveal that it can significantly increase dopamine and norepinephrine levels (Basso & Suzuki, 2017). Yet, there's more. Morning workouts help set your internal body clock (circadian rhythm) making it easier to fall asleep later at night and wake up feeling refreshed the next day.

Working out later in the day also has perks, but timing is essential. Intense exercise late at night can rev up your alertness and heart rate, making it harder to wind down for sleep. To avoid this, try to finish vigorous workouts at least three to four hours before bedtime to give your body enough time to relax and prepare for a good night's sleep. On the other hand, light to moderate evening activities, like yoga or a gentle walk, can help you relax.

So, next time you feel groggy in the morning, remember that a quick workout can lead to a more productive and emotionally balanced day.

TAKEAWAYS

- **Circadian Rhythm:** Aligning with your natural circadian rhythm supports optimal focus and energy levels.

- **Sleep:** Consistent, quality sleep is crucial for regulating the brain functions most affected by ADHD, including focus and impulse control.

- **Light Exposure:** Morning light helps synchronize the circadian rhythm, improving daytime alertness and attention.

- **Nutrition:** A well-balanced diet and the appropriate use of supplements can help reduce or manage ADHD symptoms.

- **Exercise:** Regular morning exercise boosts dopamine and norepinephrine levels improving focus and emotional balance.

Your Free Gifts

To thank you for your purchase, I'm offering you three BO-
NUSES.

To get instant access just click the link or use the QR code:

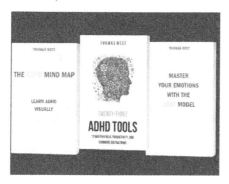

https://serenitytimelibrary.com/Men-ADHD-Free-BONUS

BONUS 1 - ADHD Toolbox: Introducing 23 powerful apps
to master focus, productivity, and eliminate distractions

BONUS 2 – The REBT Model: Teaching you simple strategies to master your emotions

BONUS 3 – The ADHD Mind Map: A visual representation of everything you need to know about ADHD

If you want to end your ADHD challenges for good and start
transforming your life, secure your copy now:

https://serenitytimelibrary.com/Men-ADHD-Free-BONUS

PART 3

Daily ADHD Challenges in Men and How to Overcome Them

Chapter 9: Thriving Professionally with ADHD

In a world that demands precision and unwavering focus, the traditional career landscape can feel treacherous for men with ADHD. Deadlines loom like thunderclouds, office politics shift like a high-stakes chess game, and even simple tasks can become insurmountable mountains. The external pressures are daunting, but the internal struggle is just as fierce. A mind teeming with ideas often stumbles in channeling that creativity into tangible results, tangled in the brambles of distraction and impulsivity. Conventional career paths, with their rigid structures, can lead to frustration and self-doubt.

Yet, within these challenges lies the potential for extraordinary success—if the right strategies and environments are chosen. This chapter explores the complexities of pursuing a career with ADHD, offering insights and tools to transform hurdles into stepping stones, helping men with ADHD not just survive, but thrive in their professional lives.

IKIGAI – FIND THE RIGHT JOB

To bring more excitement and reduce boredom in your life, schedule a dedicated time in your calendar for a 20-minute awareness exercise. During this exercise, reflect deeply on the four paths of Ikigai by answering five questions for each path. This practice can help you uncover insights about your true self and align your daily activities with your passions and strengths. Here are the questions to guide your reflection:

Path of Passion - What You Love

1. When do you feel the happiest and most content?

2. What topics or subjects could you talk about for hours?

3. Which hobbies or interests make you feel alive and fulfilled?

4. What do you love to do, even if you're not skilled yet?

5. What activities make you lose track of time because you enjoy them so much?

Path of Strength - What You're Good At

1. What achievements are you most proud of?

2. What skills or talents come naturally to you?

3. Which activities make you feel confident and capable?

4. In what areas do others often seek your advice or assistance?

5. What positive feedback do you consistently receive from others?

Path of Mission - What the World Needs

1. What changes would you like to see in the world?

2. What causes or issues are you most passionate about?

3. In what ways can your strengths and passions serve others?

4. What problems or challenges do you feel compelled to solve?

5. How do you want to contribute to your community or society?

Path of Gold - What You Can Earn Money From

1. What professions or industries excite you?

2. How can you monetize your hobbies or interests?

3. What skills or services are people willing to pay you for?

4. How do you envision making a living that aligns with your passions and strengths?

5. What steps can you take to transition from your current job to one that fulfills your Ikigai?

By dedicating this time regularly, you can gradually move toward a more exciting and less monotonous life, filling your days with energizing and inspiring activities. The Ikigai Method is a powerful starting point. Once you start developing awareness, you can complement it with practical approaches. Personality assessments, like the Myers-Briggs Type Indicator, help pinpoint your natural preferences and working styles. Career aptitude tests provide insights into fields in which your skills are most effective. Informational interviews and job shadowing offer firsthand experience in different roles.

However, if you need some inspiration, here are some career paths in which men with ADHD can thrive.

ADHD-FRIENDLY CAREERS

Creative Fields

Careers that involve innovation, creativity, and new ideas can be well-suited. These roles often allow for flexible thinking and the ability to work on diverse projects, making them engaging and fulfilling.

Related Professions

- Graphic Designer: Creating visual content for branding, advertising, and digital platforms.
- Writer/Author: Crafting stories, articles, or books in various genres and formats.
- Art Director: Leading creative advertising, publishing, and entertainment projects.

Entrepreneurial Ventures

Many successful entrepreneurs have ADHD. This might be due to their risk-taking nature, creativity, and ability to think outside the box. Entrepreneurship provides the freedom to innovate and the excitement of building something new.

Related Opportunities

- Startup Founder: Launching and managing a new business venture.
- Small Business Owner: Running a retail store, restaurant, or service-based business.
- Product Developer: Creating and bringing new products to market.

Dynamic and Fast-Paced Jobs

Jobs that offer variety, excitement, and the opportunity to take risks are often appealing. These roles involve unpredictable environments and the need for quick thinking and adaptability.

Related Professions

- Emergency Medical Technician (EMT): Providing immediate emergency medical care.

- Firefighter: Responding to fires, accidents, and other emergencies.

- Journalist: Reporting on current events, often in fast-paced and unpredictable environments.

Those are just a few examples of careers in which many individuals with ADHD are finding success and purpose. While finding an exciting job is ideal, how do you keep it?

HOW TO KEEP YOUR JOB AND GROW IN YOUR PROFESSION

Navigating the professional world can be incredibly daunting if you have ADHD. You often face unique obstacles that can make maintaining employment seem nearly impossible. These challenges result in constant frustration and anxiety; the feeling of being misunderstood and undervalued is often overwhelming. The daily struggle to stay organized, meet deadlines, and maintain focus makes you fall behind, jeopardizing your job security and professional growth. The stress of these obstacles can overshadow your talents, leaving you feeling stuck and hopeless. However, there are ways to make strategic adaptations to thrive in the workplace.

Effective Communication

Honesty and communication are crucial, but disclosing your ADHD diagnosis is not always ideal. Focus on practical solutions when discussing your strengths and weaknesses with supervisors and colleagues. For instance, if you need a quieter workspace to enhance your focus, you could say, "I've noticed that I work best in quieter environments. Could we move my desk to a less noisy area? I believe this would significantly boost my efficiency and output." Similarly, if clear deadlines help you stay on track, you might suggest, "Having clear deadlines helps me stay organized and meet my targets. Could we implement more structured timelines for our projects? I think this could improve my performance and ensure timely delivery." Share examples of past successes where similar adjustments benefited the team or the company. For instance, you could say, "When we introduced more structured deadlines in my last job, my ability to manage tasks improved, and our project completion rate increased by 15%."

By framing your requests in terms of organizational benefits, you make it easier for others to understand and support your needs.

Keeping the Job Exciting and Engaging

To maintain high productivity, the job must stay engaging and exciting. Seek new projects or responsibilities that align with your interests and strengths. For example, you could tell your boss, "I thrive on innovative tasks and have a knack for creative problem-solving. Are there any upcoming projects that could benefit from these skills? I'd love to take on more responsibility in this area to contribute more effectively to our team." This proactive approach keeps you motivated and showcases your willingness to take on challenges.

Furthermore, you can set personal milestones related to learning and skill development to stay engaged. You might discuss with your boss, "I'd like to set some personal milestones to improve my skills in data analysis over the next six months. Is there any relevant course or project that would support this goal?" This approach can improve your work experience and enhance career satisfaction and progression.

Optimizing Motivation

Creating external consequences can significantly enhance motivation, especially if you have ADHD. For instance, if regular check-ins help you work faster, proactively request them from your boss. You might say, "I've found that regular check-ins help me stay on track and meet my deadlines more efficiently. Could we schedule brief weekly meetings to review progress and set priorities?" In addition to check-ins with your boss, consider establishing peer accountability. Partner up with a colleague or friend who also seeks improved productivity. Schedule regular times to discuss your goals, progress, and any obstacles you're facing.

The ADHD ERA

If you have ADHD, conditions for success have never been so favorable. Once an elusive ideal, the four circles of Ikigai are now within reach. In the digital age, you can connect with anyone, anywhere. Even the most niche passion can find its audience, solve a problem, and become financially successful. Imagine you're passionate about astrology. In the past, reaching an audience large enough to sustain this passion would have been impossible. Now, you can apply multiple business models, like coaching or courses, and make thousands of dollars from the comfort of your sofa. Do you prefer to sell products? Today, platforms like Etsy and Amazon have changed the game. You can set up an online shop in hours and make your products available to millions worldwide. Digital marketing tools allow you to target your ideal customers while they scroll the phone from the other side of the world.

The digital landscape also offers unparalleled opportunities for personal development and learning. Platforms like Udemy, Coursera, and Khan Academy provide access to courses that can help you hone your skills or learn new ones. If you need help with organization or productivity, apps like Trello, Asana, or Notion can keep your tasks in order. You can also join online communities of individuals who share your interests and inspire you. You don't have to struggle with traditional work environments anymore. Instead, you can enjoy the flexibility that the gig economy offers. Websites like Fiverr and Upwork allow you to provide your services on your terms. Whether you're a graphic designer, writer, or consultant, you can find projects that match your skills and interests. You can now work in a way that suits your unique brain and lets you explore different paths that bring you joy and fulfillment.

The rise of remote work is another boon. The traditional 9-to-5 office job can be stifling, but working from home allows you to create an environment tailored to your needs. You can take breaks when necessary, work during peak productivity hours, and minimize distractions. This flexibility can significantly enhance your ability to focus and produce high-quality work.

Financial success no longer requires fitting into a conventional mold. The digital era celebrates uniqueness and innovation. The world is ready for your contributions, and the digital age provides all the tools you need to turn your passions into success. The best time to succeed is now. Seize it.

TAKEAWAY

1. **Ikigai Discovery Exercise**: A simple 20-minute exercise can help you discover your best opportunities. This technique, rooted in the Japanese concept of Ikigai, can guide you toward a fulfilling career path.

2. **ADHD-Friendly Careers**: Certain careers are particularly well-suited for individuals with ADHD, allowing them to leverage their unique strengths. Many people with ADHD have succeeded in these fields, turning potential challenges into advantages.

3. **Job Retention Strategies**: Effective communication and proactivity are key to keeping and growing your job. By mastering these skills, you can ensure long-term career stability and advancement.

4. **Digital Era Opportunities**: The digital era offers unprecedented opportunities for any job. This period is the best time to explore new career paths and take advantage of the vast potential of digital technology.

Chapter 10: Tools for Cultivating Healthy, Intimate Relationships

You are having a heartfelt conversation with your partner, trying to share your day. Suddenly, your partner notices that you've caught yourself drifting off, your mind racing in all directions. You snap back, only to find frustration in your partner's eyes, the moment lost, the connection frayed. The evening that started with warmth ends in icy silence or a heated argument. For men with ADHD, this scenario is all too familiar. This is just one of the many issues that can hinder the relationship.

Beyond the struggle to stay focused, others compound. It might be a temper flare-up due to a sense of rejection, the relentless need for novelty, or poor communication. These challenges create a minefield of emotions, leaving both partners hurt, misunderstood, and isolated. The frustration of trying to connect but constantly falling short can be overwhelming. The distance grows, and the once-loving partnership becomes a battleground of unmet expectations. But there's a way out. Recognizing the challenges men with ADHD face is the first step toward building stronger connections. Then, you can create more resilient relationships based on great communication and understanding.

Here are different strategies for a healthy love life.

VERBAL CUES: A SIMPLE YET TRANSFORMATIVE TOOL

The heat rises in your chest, your heart pounds faster, and a tight knot forms in your stomach as irritation or anger takes hold. When you feel the familiar surge of frustration, take a step back. Rather than speaking or acting impulsively, pause and take a deep breath. This brief moment of calm can prevent a rash response and give you the clarity to approach the situation more thoughtfully. This simple act can prevent a night spent on the sofa and is crucial for avoiding reactions that could destroy your relationship.

One powerful strategy to develop awareness and better manage emotions is the introduction of verbal cues. These cues act as signals to prevent conflicts from escalating. When either partner says the chosen word, it signals a need to take a break, breathe, and approach the conversation with a different tone. Choose a word that is easy to remember and has no negative associations, ensuring it can quickly defuse tension. Effective examples include 'pineapple' or 'marshmallow.' You can also agree on completely invented words, like "bastora" or "aprich." Don't overthink it; choose one. The word itself is a simple cue for something much bigger. It represents the effort to navigate conflicts more smoothly and maintain a positive connection.

THE ART OF APOLOGIZING

However, if you reacted impulsively despite your best efforts, all is not lost. You can master the art of apologizing to mend the situation. Learning to apologize sincerely is vital to effective communication; it should go beyond a simple "I'm sorry." Show genuine remorse and understanding of the impact of your actions. Instead of saying, "I'm sorry I got angry, but you made me mad," keep yourself accountable. Try, "I'm sorry I got angry. I see how my reaction hurt you, and I will work on managing my temper better." This kind of apology acknowledges the pain caused and demonstrates your commitment to change. When you master it, your relationship will greatly improve.

CREATING A SAFE SPACE

Setting up regular check-ins can significantly enhance communication. Weekly discussions of any lingering issues provide time for accountability and support. These sessions should be a safe space, free from judgment, where partners can openly express their needs and concerns. This practice prevents minor issues from escalating into major conflicts. Also, consider applying conflict intimacy to those meetings.

Conflict intimacy is a concept that encourages open and respectful discussions about disagreements; this approach relies on two key points:

First, both partners have valid viewpoints that deserve attention. Second, the main goal is to understand each other rather than win an argument.

Focus on active listening, acknowledge your partner's feelings, and find common ground. For instance, if you disagree about household chores, resist insisting on your viewpoint. Instead, try to understand your partner's perspective and work together to find a compromise.

REJECTION SENSITIVE DYSPHORIA: THE HIDDEN HEARTACHE

Rejection Sensitive Dysphoria (RSD) is another hidden yet profound challenge for men with ADHD. Criticism and rejection can create intense pain and emotional turmoil, even if unintended or minor. This hypersensitivity can lead to overreactions, withdrawal, and fear of disappointing your partner. The constant dread of rejection creates a barrier to open communication, making it hard to feel secure in the relationship and your partner may feel they are walking on eggshells, unsure what might trigger an emotional outburst. Therefore, they retreat into silence.

One effective strategy to address RSD is establishing a clear and compassionate communication plan. Encourage your partner to express their feelings and concerns gently. Ask them to use "I" statements to minimize feelings of blame. For instance, saying, "I feel worried when you don't respond" instead of "You never listen to me" can help reduce the emotional sting. Another example could be, "I feel hurt when plans change suddenly" rather than "You always cancel on me." This fosters a supportive environment instead of assigning blame.

Practicing self-awareness and self-compassion is also crucial. When you feel the sting of perceived rejection, take a moment to pause and reassess the situation objectively. Remember that your partner's feedback is not a personal attack. A straightforward method to implement this is to shift your mindset using a mental mantra, such as "This is about growth, not hurt." Keeping a journal can also be beneficial. Reflect daily on your interactions, noting instances where you felt rejected or overly sensitive. You will better understand your triggers and respond rationally in the future. For example, you might feel rejected when your partner is busy. Prepare mentally for these moments; remember that their busyness does not reflect their feelings for you.

A NEED FOR NOVELTY

For men with ADHD, the need for novelty can be both a blessing and a curse. The initial thrill of a new relationship is rich with spontaneous adventures and fresh experiences. It perfectly satisfies the craving for stimulation. However, as the relationship settles into a routine, this need for novelty can become a source of restlessness and dissatisfaction. The once electrifying connection may now feel mundane, prompting the temptation to seek new thrills elsewhere. This can create a painful disconnect where one partner feels unfulfilled, and the other feels inadequate or unappreciated. It's essential to inject variety and excitement into the relationship.

One effective solution is to plan regular date nights with a twist. Try new activities together, such as cooking a new cuisine, taking a dance class, or exploring a new hiking trail. These shared experiences can reignite the spark and provide the novelty that keeps the ADHD brain engaged. Additionally, surprise your partner with spontaneous gestures of love and appreciation. It could be as simple as leaving a heartfelt note, planning a surprise weekend getaway, or trying a new hobby together.

Also, consider setting mutual goals that require teamwork and creativity. It could be anything: planning a dream vacation, starting a home improvement project, or training for a marathon. A new sense of purpose and excitement grows in the relationship when you have a shared mission. This strengthens the bond through collaboration and shared achievements. Therefore, embrace and nurture the desire for novelty rather than pushing it away. Transform it from a potential source of conflict into a dynamic force, keeping the relationship vibrant and alive.

While ADHD presents challenges to communication and intimacy, you can overcome these obstacles. You can develop a healthy relationship by setting improvements like verbal cues and regular check-ins. A relationship where you and your partner feel understood, valued, and deeply connected. Remember, the goal is not perfection but progress towards a closer bond.

TAKEAWAYS

1. **Impact of Miscommunication:** Beyond inattentiveness, issues like temper flare-ups and poor communication compound the difficulties. These challenges can leave both partners feeling hurt and isolated.

2. **Verbal Cues:** Introducing verbal cues can help manage emotions and prevent conflicts from escalating. Choose a word that signals the need to pause and reset the conversation.

3. **The Art of Apologizing:** Sincere apologies are vital for mending impulsive reactions. Acknowledge the impact of your actions and show genuine remorse.

4. **Regular Check-Ins:** Weekly discussions of any lingering issues can enhance communication. These sessions should be judgment-free zones where both partners can express their needs.

5. **Rejection Sensitive Dysphoria:** RSD can lead to over-reactions and emotional turmoil. Establishing compassionate communication can help reduce the emotional sting of perceived rejection.

6. **The Need for Novelty in Relationships:** For men with ADHD, the craving for novelty can lead to restlessness in relationships. Inject variety and excitement to keep the connection vibrant and alive.

7. **Building a Healthy Relationship:** Implement strategies like verbal cues and regular check-ins to overcome

ADHD-related challenges. Focus on progress and fostering a closer bond with your partner.

Chapter 11: Managing Money and Family Responsibilities

You're standing at the checkout line of your favorite electronics store. Bright overhead lights and the hum of conversations fill the space. You feel the weight of the day lifting as you browse the items near the register. The shelves are lined with tempting, last-minute buys—colorful phone accessories, sleek headphones, and various gadgets. Suddenly, a flashy multi-functional tool catches your eye. It's elegant, with shiny metal parts, and promises to make your life easier. The packaging boasts a myriad of features: it's a bottle opener, a screwdriver, a flashlight, and more. You pick it up, feeling its weight in your hand, imagining the convenience it will bring. A surge of excitement courses through you, wiping away any second thoughts. You imagine how impressed your friends will be when you whip it out at the next gathering. Without a second thought, you swipe your card. The cashier smiles and hands you the bag, and you feel a momentary rush of satisfaction. You walk out of the store, the evening air hitting your face, and head home, still basking in the glow of your latest acquisition.

Later that evening, you sit down in your living room. The TV is on, but your attention drifts to the growing pile of similar gadgets on your coffee table and shelves. The excitement fades as reality sets in. You already have several tools that serve the same purpose and are collecting dust. The new gadget, once so appealing, now seems redundant. Guilt and frustration bubble up as you realize this impulsive purchase, like many others before it, was unnecessary. You are left questioning why you bought it in the first place and how much money you've wasted on similar whims.

The thrill of instant gratification often overshadows the long-term consequences, making saving and budgeting difficult. The financial impact of impulsivity is profound. Each spontaneous purchase, while seemingly minor in isolation, accumulates over time. This disrupts budgeting efforts as money intended for essential expenses goes into impulsive buys. The cycle of impulsivity can also result in credit card debt, as the ease of swiping a card can mask the reality of overspending. Interest and late fees compound the problem, making it harder to pay off balances and creating a debt spiral that feels impossible to escape.

This behavior often stems from an attempt to cope with the stress and demands of daily life. The fleeting pleasure of a new purchase provides a temporary escape, but it's a double-edged sword. Guilt and anxiety quickly replace immediate gratification, creating a vicious cycle of emotional spending.

THE COST OF PROCRASTINATION

Procrastination compounds financial difficulties, creating a perfect storm of stress and disorganization. Picture a stack of bills and a cluttered desk, each unpaid invoice a glaring reminder of the tasks you've put off. Procrastination in financial matters often starts with minor delays. It might be postponing the payment of a bill, putting off checking your bank statements, or delaying setting up a budget. These minor deferrals can snowball into significant issues. Bills go unpaid, leading to late fees and higher interest rates. Important financial documents get lost in the clutter, and you might miss payment deadlines. The consequences of procrastination extend beyond the immediate financial penalties as the mental burden of unresolved financial issues can lead to a cycle of avoidance. The stress of dealing with finances becomes overwhelming, and further procrastination is the only way to escape.

This avoidance can result in a lack of financial oversight, leading to a lack of awareness of your income, expenses, or debt levels. This lack of clarity makes planning for the future and setting realistic financial goals nearly impossible.

Society often expects men to be the financial bedrock of their families. Bills spread out before you, and the weight of expectation bears on your shoulders as you sit at the kitchen table. The house is quiet, but the pressure is palpable. You feel the unspoken demand to ensure you pay every bill on time, every expense is accounted for, and every financial decision is flawlessly executed.

This responsibility is more than just balancing a checkbook; it's about providing security and stability for your loved ones. The mortgage payment ensures a roof over your family's heads. The grocery bill puts food on the table. The utility payments keep the lights on and the home warm. You stretch each dollar to cover the necessities and the unexpected expenses that life throws your way—car repairs, medical bills, or school supplies for your children. The pressure to be the perfect provider can feel relentless. There's an underlying fear of failure that gnaws at you—what if you can't make ends meet this month? What if an unexpected expense derails your budget? This fear can lead to sleepless nights and constant anxiety. A nagging worry that you're not living up to societal expectations or your family's needs.

Moreover, this pressure can create a sense of isolation. Financial struggles are often kept private, compounding the feeling that you must bear this burden alone. The silence surrounding financial worries can be deafening, making it difficult to seek help or admit when you're struggling. You might feel like you're walking a tightrope, with any misstep leading to financial ruin, and this fear of falling can be paralyzing.

Acknowledging these feelings and addressing the underlying issues is crucial. The first step is recognizing the immense pressure and the emotional toll it takes. It's important to understand that you're not alone in this struggle and can manage these expectations. Also, there are strategies to help you build a more secure financial future for yourself and your family.

THE 50/30/20 STRATEGY – FINANCIAL FREEDOM

As management expert Peter Drucker famously said, "What gets measured gets managed."

This principle is particularly true when it comes to managing your finances. One effective strategy to help you stay on top of your money is the 50/30/20 strategy. This rule clearly outlines how to balance financial responsibilities with personal desires.

To implement the 50/30/20 strategy, follow these five steps:

1. Calculate Your Income
   Start by determining your total monthly income after taxes. This is the amount you have available to allocate according to the 50/30/20 strategy. Include all sources of income, such as your salary, side gigs, and any other regular earnings.

2. Allocate 50% to Necessities
   Half of your income should go towards essential living expenses. These include rent or mortgage payments, utilities, groceries, transportation, insurance, and other non-negotiable bills. To make this easier, list all your essential expenses and total them. If your essential costs exceed 50% of your income, look for ways to reduce them. This might require you to reduce utility usage or find more affordable housing.

3. Dedicate 30% to Discretionary Spending
   The following 30% of your income relates to things that enhance your lifestyle but aren't strictly necessary. This includes dining out, entertainment, hobbies, travel, and other personal indulgences. To apply this, track your discretionary spending for a month to see where your money goes. Then, a budget for each category should be set within this 30% allocation. This step ensures you can enjoy life without overspending.

4. Save and Repay Debt with 20%
   The remaining 20% is for savings and debt repayment. This includes building an emergency fund, contributing to retirement accounts, and paying down credit card balances. It's also for savings related to future goals like buying a home or vacation. To make this more actionable, automate your savings and debt payments. Set up automatic transfers to your savings accounts and for your debts. This ensures consistency and removes the temptation to spend this money elsewhere.

5. Adjust and Monitor Regularly
   Life circumstances change, and so should your budget. Review your spending and income regularly to ensure you apply the 50/30/20 strategy. Use budgeting apps like Mint, YNAB, or PocketGuard to track your progress. These tools categorize expenses, provide insights into your spending habits, and help you adjust your allocations.

By following the 50/30/20 rule, you can achieve a balanced approach to managing your money. This method ensures you cover your essential needs, enjoy life, and save for the future.

THE 24-HOUR RULE

Implement the "24-hour rule." When you feel the urge to make an impulsive purchase, wait 24 hours before buying it. This pause allows you to evaluate whether the purchase is essential or just a fleeting desire. To make the 24-hour rule easier to apply, follow these nine steps:

1. Set a Reminder
   As soon as you feel the urge to buy something, set a reminder on your phone or write a note to revisit the purchase in 24 hours. This physical or digital prompt serves as a commitment to yourself to think it through.

2. Create a Wishlist
   Instead of immediately buying, add the item to a Wishlist—either on the store's website, in a dedicated app, or on paper. This allows you to acknowledge your desire without acting on it immediately.

3. Reflect on the Purchase
   During the 24 hours, take a few moments to consider the following questions:
   - Do I really need this item, or do I just want it?
   - Do I already have something similar at home?

- Will this purchase add value to my life, or is it a temporary thrill?
- Can I afford this right now without compromising other financial priorities?

4. Consult a Trusted Person

   Talk to a friend or family member about the potential purchase. Sometimes, verbalizing your thoughts can help clarify your decision. Their perspective might offer valuable insights you hadn't considered.

5. Review Your Budget

   Check your budget to see how this purchase fits your financial plan. If it means diverting money from essentials or savings, it's probably not worth it. Use this time to ensure that your spending aligns with your financial goals.

6. Evaluate Alternatives

   Consider if there are less expensive or free alternatives. Maybe you can borrow the item, find it on sale later, or realize you don't need it at all.

7. Final Decision

   After 24 hours, reassess your desire to purchase the item. You will have a clearer perspective on whether the item is truly worth buying.

By applying the 24-hour rule, you can develop better spending habits and make more thoughtful financial decisions. This simple strategy can help curb impulsive buys, ensuring that your purchases are deliberate and aligned with your financial well-being.

PLAN YOUR FINANCIAL FUTURE IN 7 STEPS

"If you fail to plan, you are planning to fail." - Benjamin Franklin.

Whether you want to buy a house, start a business, or save for retirement, a solid financial plan is essential.

1. Define Your Goal
   Identify your financial goal. Make it specific and measurable. For example, instead of saying, "I want to save money," say, "I want to save $10,000 for a down payment on a house within three years."

2. Determine Your Monthly Contribution
   Establish a realistic timeline for achieving your goal. Break it down into smaller milestones if necessary. For example, if your goal is to save $10,000 in three years, aim to save approximately $278 per month. Choose an amount you can afford without compromising your essential expenses or financial stability.

3. Assess Your Current Situation

   Take stock of your current financial status. List your income sources, monthly expenses, savings, and debts. This will give you a clear picture of your financial situation.

4. Open a Dedicated

   AccountSet up a separate savings account for your goal. This will help keep the funds distinct from your everyday spending and reduce the temptation to dip into them.

5. Automate Your Savings

   Set automatic monthly transfers from your checking account to your dedicated savings account. This ensures consistency and makes saving a part of your routine without requiring constant attention.

6. Monitor and Adjust

   Regularly review your progress towards your goal. Use budgeting apps to track your savings and spending. Adjust your plan to stay on track, whether increasing your monthly savings or extending your timeline.

7. Stay Motivated

   Keep your goal in mind and celebrate small milestones along the way. Visual reminders such as a picture of the house you want to buy, can help keep you motivated.

By following these steps, you can create a practical and achievable financial plan, bringing your goals within reach.

Addressing impulsivity and procrastination requires a proactive approach to financial management. Recognizing how ADHD affects your finances is the first step toward change. Implementing the strategies and tools presented will pave the way for a more secure financial future.

Next, we will move to Chapter 12 to create a personalized organizational system. This system will help you manage your time, prioritize tasks, and maintain an orderly environment that supports your productivity and well-being.

TAKEAWAYS

1. **Societal Expectations and Financial Pressure** Men often feel the burden of being the financial providers for their families, adding to stress and anxiety. This pressure can lead to isolation, as financial struggles are frequently kept private, intensifying the sense of responsibility.

2. **Procrastination:** It can lead to late fees, higher interest rates, and significant stress. Unpaid bills and a lack of financial oversight contribute to a cycle of avoidance, making it difficult to plan and achieve financial goals.

3. **The 50/30/20 Strategy:** It helps balance financial responsibilities by allocating 50% of income to necessities, 30% to discretionary spending, and 20% to savings and debt repayment.

4. **The 24-Hour Rule:** Implement the "24-hour rule" to avoid impulsive purchases. By waiting 24 hours before buying, you can evaluate if the purchase is necessary and fits within your budget, reducing unnecessary spending.

5. **Planning Your Financial Future:** Define specific financial goals, determine monthly contributions, assess your current situation, and automate your savings to achieve financial stability and reach your objectives.

Chapter 12: Crafting an Organization System for ADHD

Imagine waking up to a serene and organized space. Your keys are right where you left them, your clothes are neatly arranged, and your workspace is ready for a productive day. This isn't just a dream; it's a reality you can achieve with focused effort. Decluttering isn't just about cleaning up; it's about reclaiming your environment so it works for you, not against you. The benefits are clear: reduced stress, improved focus, and a sense of calm and readiness. Clutter is a common enemy for many, but for those with ADHD, it can feel like an impossible challenge. The visual chaos of a cluttered space is a constant source of distraction, making it even harder to focus on tasks at hand. Every misplaced item is a reminder of an unfinished task, creating mental clutter that amplifies stress and anxiety.

We've all been there; the frustration of wanting to start a task but getting sidetracked by the disorder around us. If you have ADHD, this is a daily struggle. You might begin your day with the intention of being productive, only to spend the first hour just clearing a space to work. This cycle is not just exhausting; it's demoralizing. It can make you feel like you're constantly playing catch-up. Clutter isn't just a nuisance—it's a barrier to living an organized, fulfilling life. The constant presence of disarray can lead to feelings of guilt, shame, and even helplessness. You might look around at your space and wonder why keeping things in order is so hard when others seem to manage just fine.

This isn't just about tidiness; it's about the impact clutter has on your ability to think clearly, stay focused, and find peace in your home.

The emotional toll is real. The mess around you reflects the chaos inside your mind, and the constant struggle to maintain order can be overwhelming. This cycle feeds on itself, creating more stress, more distractions, and more clutter. But it doesn't have to be this way. This chapter aims to help you break free from the clutter and create a space that supports your goals and well-being. There are specific, actionable steps you can take to reclaim your environment and live a more organized, fulfilling life.

Step 1: Clear Your Entryway – The Launchpad of Your Day

The entryway is the first place you see when you come home and the last place you pass through before leaving. It's also a notorious clutter magnet, with shoes, bags, mail, and keys often strewn about. For men with ADHD, this area can become a significant source of daily frustration, leading to rushed exits and lost items. Here are some options to consider:

- Designate specific spots for daily items
- Invest in a small table or wall-mounted shelf near the door
- Place a bowl or tray for keys, wallet, and essentials
- Install hooks on the wall for coat and bag
- Consider a small basket for incoming mail, and make it a rule to sort through it weekly

As you implement these changes, be consistent in using these designated spots. The key is repetition—every time you come home, make it a habit to place your items in their designated spots. This simple system will help reduce morning chaos and ensure that your essentials are always within reach.

Step 2: Tackle the Closet

Closets can easily become overwhelming, filled with clothes you no longer wear, single shoes, and lost accessories. For individuals with ADHD, the disorder of a disorganized closet can make getting dressed in the morning a time-consuming challenge.

Start by taking everything out of your closet so you can see all of your clothes and decide what to keep. Ask yourself if you've worn each item in the past year. If not, it's time to let it go. Group similar items together, such as shirts, pants, and jackets. Consider using slim hangers to save space and keep things neat. Organize your clothes by type and color, and keep the items you wear most often within easy reach. You can also use shelves or baskets at the bottom of the closet for shoes.

Make it a habit to keep your closet organized. Every time you do laundry, take a minute to put things back where they belong. If something is consistently out of place, re-evaluate your system and make adjustments. The goal is to create a closet that works for you, making it easier to get dressed and reducing clutter-related stress.

Step 3: Streamline Your Workspace

A cluttered workspace is a major distraction, especially when your mind is already prone to wandering. Piles of papers, scattered office supplies, and general disorder can make it nearly impossible to focus on the task at hand.

Start by clearing everything off your desk. Wipe down the surface to create a fresh, clean slate. As you begin to put things back, think carefully about what you actually need on a daily basis. Keep only the essentials within arm's reach—your computer, a notepad, a pen, and perhaps a small organizer for other frequently used items. Designate specific areas for different types of work. For instance, keep a filing system nearby for papers you need to reference regularly, but avoid letting them pile up on your desk. Consider investing in a few desk organizers—trays, pen holders, and cable management systems—to keep everything tidy and in place.

Make it a habit to clear your desk at the end of each day. Even if you've only used a few items, taking just a few minutes to tidy up will make a big difference in maintaining a clutter-free workspace. The key is consistency—if you make decluttering part of your daily routine, it will become second nature, and your workspace will remain a place of focus and productivity.

Step 4: Declutter the Kitchen

The kitchen is often the heart of the home, but for men with ADHD, it can quickly become a source of stress if it's disorganized. Cluttered countertops, overstuffed cabinets, and misplaced cooking tools can turn meal prep into a chaotic experience.

Here are some options to consider:

Start by focusing on your countertops. Clear everything off and only put back the items you use daily, such as a coffee maker, toaster, or a bowl of fruit. Store less frequently used appliances in cabinets to free up space.

Next, tackle your cabinets. Begin by sorting through your pantry items, check expiration dates, and get rid of anything that's past its prime. Group similar items together—canned goods, grains, snacks—and use baskets or clear containers to keep things organized and easy to see. For cooking tools, consider hanging a pegboard on the wall or installing drawer dividers to keep utensils sorted and accessible.

Finally, make it a habit to clean as you go when cooking. Instead of letting dirty dishes pile up, wash them or load them into the dishwasher as you prepare your meal.

At the end of each day, take a few minutes to wipe down countertops and put everything back in its place. A clean, organized kitchen will make cooking more enjoyable and reduce the stress of meal prep.

Step 5: Simplify the Bedroom – Create a Restful Sanctuary

Your bedroom should be a place of rest and relaxation, but when it's cluttered, it can feel anything but peaceful. Clothes on the floor, nightstands overflowing with items, and an unmade bed can all contribute to a sense of unease and difficulty winding down.

Start with your bed. Make it every morning. This small action sets the tone for the rest of your day and instantly makes the room feel more orderly.

Next, clear off your nightstands, leaving only the essentials— perhaps a lamp, a book, and a glass of water. Store anything else in drawers or on shelves to keep surfaces clutter-free.

Move on to your clothes. If you haven't already tackled your closet, now is the time. Ensure that all your clothes have a home, whether it's in a drawer, on a hanger, or in a laundry basket. Consider adding a chair or a bench to place clothes you plan to wear again rather than tossing them on the floor.

Finally, create a nightly routine to maintain your bedroom's calm atmosphere. Spend just a few minutes each evening putting things back in their place—folding clothes, clearing off surfaces, and tidying up. This routine will help you wind down and pre-pare for a restful night's sleep, and you'll wake up to a serene and inviting bedroom.

Step 6: Organize Your Digital Space

Digital clutter can be just as overwhelming as physical clutter. An overflowing inbox, a chaotic desktop, and disorganized files can all contribute to feelings of stress and distraction.

Start with your desktop. Clear off all unnecessary icons, leaving only the folders and files you use regularly. Create a system of folders for different types of documents—work, personal, projects, etc.—and stick to it. This will make it easier to find what you need and keep your digital space tidy.

Next, tackle your email inbox. Begin by unsubscribing from newsletters and promotions you no longer read. Then, sort through your emails, deleting what you don't need and organizing the rest into folders. Aim to keep your inbox as empty as possible, dealing with emails as they come in rather than letting them pile up.

Finally, organize your files. Whether they're on your computer, in the cloud, or on external drives, create a consistent filing system that works for you. Label folders clearly and make it a habit to save new files in the correct place immediately.

To maintain your digital space, set aside time each week to tidy up—delete old files, organize your documents, and clear out your inbox. This will help prevent digital clutter from building up and keep your mind clear and focused.

TAKEAWAYS

1. **A Daily Battle with Disorganization**: Cluttered spaces and scattered thoughts can amplify stress, hinder productivity, and affect mental well-being.

2. **Decluttering is more than just tidying up**: It's about creating an environment that supports your goals and helps you manage the challenges of ADHD.

3. **Start Small**: Begin with manageable areas to build momentum and make the decluttering process less overwhelming.

4. **Designate Spaces**: Assign specific spots for everyday items to minimize stress and create a more organized environment.

5. **Simplify Your Surroundings**: Reduce clutter by keeping only the essentials, making it easier to maintain order over time.

6. **Establish Routines**: Implement daily or weekly tidying routines to prevent clutter from accumulating and to maintain a clear, focused space.

7. **Tailor Systems to Your Needs**: Create organizational systems that align with your natural habits, making them easier to maintain and more effective for your lifestyle.

PART 4

CBT-Based Training for Executive Functions

As we saw, ADHD impacts the prefrontal cortex, which affects executive functions such as working memory, emotional regulation, and planning. In the following chapters, you'll discover a comprehensive 6-week training program designed to support and enhance these executive functions. This program will help you improve time management, eliminate anxious thoughts, and develop a comprehensive plan from start to finish.

Chapter 13: Finding Strength in Your Diagnosis

The moment you receive an ADHD diagnosis as an adult, a whirlwind of emotions can sweep through your mind. Regret might mix with relief as you realize the past challenges were not due to a lack of effort or willpower. This understanding can be liberating but also daunting, marking the beginning of a journey toward self-improvement. In this first week, the goal is to come to terms with your diagnosis and commit to personal development.

THE REFLECTION JOURNAL (WEEK 1)

The Reflection Journal is not a simple notebook; it's a sacred space for your thoughts and emotions. This tool will help you track patterns, identify triggers, and celebrate victories, making the abstract tangible and the overwhelming manageable. As you write, you will begin to see your journey unfold, each entry a stepping stone towards greater awareness.

Here are the four steps to use it effectively:

1. Daily Writing Practice
    Set aside 10-15 minutes daily to write in your journal. Find a quiet, comfortable space free from distractions. This is your time to connect with yourself, so make it a ritual you look forward to.

2. Exploring Your Diagnosis

   Start by writing about your feelings regarding your ADHD diagnosis. Don't filter your thoughts; let them flow naturally. Reflect on how this diagnosis has influenced your daily life. What challenges do you face? What unexpected positives have come to light?

3. Delving Into Emotions

   Pay attention to your emotions as you write. Are there feelings of frustration, relief, or sadness? Dig deep into these emotions. Understanding your emotional landscape is the first step toward managing it effectively.

4. A Bright Future

   Write your goals for this program. What would you like to achieve? How would you like to feel?

By dedicating time to this practice, you will begin to see patterns and gain insights into how ADHD affects you. This is crucial for understanding your symptoms and developing strategies to manage them.

3 STEPS TO IDENTIFY STRENGTHS AND RESOURCES (WEEK 1)

Acknowledging your diagnosis is only part of the journey. The next step is to recognize and harness your inherent strengths and available resources. This is where the Strengths and Resources Inventory comes into play.

1. Listing Personal Strengths

    Take your time to reflect on your strengths. Write down at least five qualities that you consider your assets. Do you have a knack for creativity, a resilient spirit, or an empathetic nature? These are your superpowers, tools you can wield in your daily life. If you need guided assistance finding your strengths, use free resources like the VIA Character Strengths.

2. Recognizing Resources

    Think about the resources at your disposal. These can be supportive friends or family members and books that offer wisdom. However, do not limit yourself to the "real" world. If you cannot find support within your circle, join online forums and connect with others facing similar challenges. Finally, consider the opportunity to work with professionals like therapists and coaches.

3. Reflection and Application

   Once you have your lists, reflect on how these strengths and resources can support your growth. For instance, if creativity is one of your strengths, consider how you can incorporate innovative solutions into your life. If you have supportive friends, think about how to lean on them when you need encouragement. By identifying and acknowledging your strengths and resources, you empower yourself. This inventory becomes a toolkit you can draw from whenever you face challenges, reminding you that you are ready to handle them.

Change can be uncomfortable, but it is essential for growth. Embrace it with an open mind and a positive attitude. Understand that setbacks are a natural part of the journey; instead of viewing them as failures, see them as opportunities to learn and improve. Commit to lifelong learning and self-improvement by seeking new strategies to manage ADHD. Be open to trying different approaches, and remember that growth is not about achieving perfection but making progress.

As you begin this program, understand that you are not alone. This first session marks the start of a transformative journey. By accepting your diagnosis, leveraging your strengths, and committing to continuous growth, you are paving the way for success. Stay dedicated to your practices, keep an open heart and mind, and believe in your potential. The road ahead may have challenges, but with each step, you move closer to a more fulfilling and empowered life.

TAKEAWAYS

1. **The ADHD Diagnosis**: Receiving an ADHD diagnosis as an adult can evoke a mix of regret and relief. Embrace this understanding as a liberating and daunting start to self-improvement.

2. **Enhancing Self-Awareness**: The program's first week focuses on improving self-awareness and helping you to recognize strengths and weaknesses and their impact on others.

3. **Reflection Journal:** The Reflection Journal is a dedicated space for your thoughts and emotions. Spend 10-15 minutes daily in a quiet space to connect with yourself. Write about your feelings regarding your ADHD diagnosis, exploring challenges and positives.

Chapter 14: Managing Time Effectively

Ever feel like your day disappears before you know it?

If you have ADHD, this struggle is way too familiar, marked by the constant battle against time blindness and the chaos it brings. In Chapter 4, you discovered how bad working memory can distort your perception of time, making it challenging to stay on top of tasks. In Week 2, you will tackle this with practical tools and exercises. They aim to sharpen your time awareness and enhance your scheduling skills.

One key integration is the use of a visible timer. It is crucial to provide a visual representation of the passing minutes, helping to ground your sense of time and keep you focused on tasks.

TIME AUDIT WORKSHEET (W2)

The first tool in this journey toward mastering time is the Time Audit Worksheet. Think of it as a mirror reflecting your daily habits and routines, clearly showing where your time truly goes. The Time Audit Worksheet is a simple yet powerful tool. It's a log where you'll track your activities throughout the day, capturing start and end times for each task.

For one week, write down everything you do each day. Be meticulous; record even the seemingly insignificant activities and note the start and end times of each task. Use the Pomodoro

Technique at the end of each 30-minute session, and log the activities you worked on during that period. This ensures you keep a detailed and accurate record of your productivity. At the end of the week, review your entries. Look for patterns—how much time do you spend on work, leisure, commuting, or distractions? Identify areas where you could manage time more effectively.

Time Activity

8-8.30 Walk and shower

8.30-9 Breakfast

9-9.30 Replying to emails

9.30-10 Replying to emails and social media

10-10.30 Meeting with client

As you complete this exercise, you might not believe your findings. You may discover that what seems like a quick social media check takes an hour or that minor interruptions accumulate significant chunks of wasted time. This awareness is the first step toward change.

PLANNER (W2)

This tool helps translate your newfound time awareness into actionable schedules. A planner or digital calendar is your roadmap for each day, week, and month. Whether you prefer the tactile feel of paper or the convenience of digital apps, the key is consistency in usage.

Select a planner or calendar app that suits your style. Some prefer the simplicity of a physical planner, while others might opt for digital apps like Google Calendar or Todoist. Every evening, spend 5 minutes planning your following day: schedule tasks, appointments, and even breaks. Be realistic about the time needed for each activity. Throughout the day, review your schedule. Adjust as needed, but stick to your plan as closely as possible. Imagine your planner or calendar as the architect of your day, laying down a blueprint for success. By planning, you're less likely to be caught off guard by unexpected tasks and more likely to use your time efficiently.

In Chapter 17, we'll explore planning in more depth. For now, externalize tasks, practice, and get comfortable with tools such as Google Calendar. Like any skill, time management requires regular and consistent effort to master. Here are a few tips to help you along the way:

- Start Small
  Don't overwhelm yourself by trying to overhaul your entire routine overnight. Begin with minor changes, such as tracking your time for a few key activities or planning a single day in detail.

- Be Honest
  When using the Time Audit Worksheet, be honest with yourself. The goal is to understand your current habits

without judgment, providing a foundation for improvement.

- Stay Flexible
  Life is unpredictable, and plans can change. Adaptability is crucial. If something unexpected comes up, adjust your schedule and move forward without frustration.

- Celebrate Progress
  Acknowledge your successes, no matter how small. Each step toward better time management is a victory worth celebrating.

Remember, the journey to mastering time management is ongoing. It requires patience, practice, and persistence. Yet, with the right tools and a commitment to change, you can transform how you interact with time, leading to a more organized and productive life. Through these exercises, you will master the art of effective scheduling. Soon, the stress and frustration of feeling perpetually behind will disappear.

Looking ahead to Week 3, you will build on this foundation by exploring strategies to make tasks manageable. You will learn how to approach daily responsibilities, turning hours into a series of achievable goals and rewarding milestones.

TASK BREAKDOWN (W3)

How do you eat an airplane?

It might seem like a riddle, but for Michael Lotito, this was a genuine challenge he enthusiastically undertook. Known as Mr. Eat-All, Lotito was a French entertainer with an extraordinary talent: he could consume inedible objects. Nothing showcased his unique ability more dramatically than when he decided to eat an airplane. Between 1978 and 1980, Lotito devoured a Cessna 150, transforming the seemingly impossible into reality.

How did he do it?

Well, one piece at a time. Just like eating an airplane, achieving monumental tasks can seem overwhelming if viewed in their entirety. However, if you break down the goal into manageable tasks, you can conquer even the most daunting challenge. Each step you take leads to progress, and soon, the once-impossible task becomes an accomplished reality. Lotito's story is a testament to the power of perseverance and the effectiveness of a step-by-step approach.

Invest the third week in learning this powerful tool. First, select a significant task you must complete. This could be anything from finishing a work project to organizing your garage. Let's say you must prepare a presentation for an upcoming meeting. Due to its scope and importance, this task might feel overwhelming at first glance.

Then, break it down. Divide the large task into smaller, more manageable steps. This process reduces anxiety and makes the task less intimidating. For the presentation, break it down into steps such as:

1. Designing the slides

2. Creating an outline

3. Researching the topic

4. Practicing the presentation

Once you have the steps, apply sequential order and define the next to complete. This visual representation allows you to see the progression and better manage time.

On your Task Breakdown Sheet, it might look like this:

- Research the topic (Day 1)
- Create an outline (Day 2)
- Design the slides (Days 3-4)
- Practice the presentation (Day 5)

Before we delve into the specifics of planning (Chapter 17), it's essential to become familiar with the overall process. Start developing the skills to recall activities involved in larger projects and accurately predict completion times. Without those foundational skills, even the most detailed planning approaches will fail due to a lack of solid groundwork.

The next tool is an evergreen approach to prioritization, a vital aspect of effective task management.

THE EISENHOWER MATRIX (W3)

Imagine holding an empty glass jar. This jar represents your daily schedule—your time and energy for a single day. You must carefully decide what to put into this jar to make the most of each day.

First, identify the critical tasks, those that truly matter and have the most significant impact on your day. They are like large rocks. Picture these rocks as specific, tangible things. One might be a project deadline at work—a sturdy, angular stone representing the focus and effort required to complete it. Another rock could be a workout session, depicted as a smooth, rounded stone, symbolizing the health and energy it brings you. These rocks represent the non-negotiable tasks you must accomplish to ensure a successful day. Next, consider the small but still significant activities that fill your day. These are the pebbles. Maybe one pebble is the meeting with a colleague, one is a grocery shopping trip, and one is catching up on household chores. Picture the pebbles as colorful, polished stones, small enough to fit in your hand yet significant enough to require attention. When you add these pebbles to the jar, they fill the spaces around the big rocks. Finally, consider the sand. The sand represents minor tasks and distractions that can fill your day. The time you invest in answering emails, browsing social media, or dealing with unexpected interruptions. Imagine the sand as fine grains sparkling under the light. When you pour it into the jar, it flows into the nooks and crannies left between the rocks and pebbles, filling every available space.

Here is the crucial part: If you start your day by filling the jar with sand, you will not have room for pebbles and rocks. The least significant activities steal the space of the essential tasks, leading to unproductive days. Instead, prioritize your main tasks. Then, attend to the smaller but necessary pebbles and allow the sand to fill the remaining gaps. It is a practical reminder that focusing on what truly matters ensures the effective use of your time.

The Eisenhower Matrix is a powerful tool that categorizes tasks based on urgency and importance, helping you visualize and prioritize your workload. Picture a simple box divided into four quadrants. By listing your tasks in these quadrants, you gain clarity on what needs immediate attention and what you can defer or delegate. This visual organization turns a chaotic task list into a clear, actionable plan, allowing you to work effectively. It boosts productivity and reduces stress, helping you start your day with a clear and focused mind.

During the fourth week, take each morning to create a list of tasks you need to accomplish and use the Matrix to determine their order. This method ensures your to-do list is a carefully curated plan of action, not just a random collection of tasks. As you check off each completed task, you track your progress, providing a sense of accomplishment and motivation.

The Matrix: Draw a box divided into four quadrants. Label them as follows:

1. Quadrant 1: Urgent & Important

2. Quadrant 2: Not Urgent & Important

3. Quadrant 3: Urgent & Not Important

4. Quadrant 4: Not Urgent & Not Important

Then, list all your tasks. This can include work assignments, personal errands, and any other responsibilities. Once you have your list, place each task in the appropriate quadrant.

Q1 - Urgent & Important: These tasks require immediate action and have significant consequences, such as meeting a project deadline or addressing a health issue. They are critical to your immediate well-being and success. By addressing these first, you prevent crises and reduce stress.

Q2 - Not Urgent & Important: Crucial tasks that do not need immediate attention, such as researching and setting up a retirement savings plan, often contribute to long-term success and fulfillment. By scheduling these activities, you ensure continuous progress.

Q3 - Urgent & Not Important: Tasks such as attending a non-critical meeting or responding to certain emails might demand immediate attention but are optional. You can often delegate or manage those tasks with less personal involvement.

Q4 - Not Urgent & Not Important: You can minimize or eliminate them. Examples are excessive social media browsing or watching TV. They often act as distractions and consume valuable time without providing any real benefit.

By implementing this tool, you will no longer feel overwhelmed by the sheer volume of things to do. Instead, you will have a clear, manageable plan, allowing you to tackle tasks efficiently. The Eisenhower Matrix is the key to unlocking a more organized, productive, and stress-free life. Imagine ending your day with a sense of achievement, knowing you made significant progress toward your goals.

Looking to week 4, you will learn how to overcome Emotional Obstacles. While task management is essential, we must address the emotional hurdles that often accompany ADHD. You will discover a powerful tool to manage stress, anxiety, and emotional downs. By combining time management tools with emotional resilience techniques, you will increase both productivity and self-regulation.

As you incorporate these strategies into your daily routine, remember that perfection is not the goal. The objective is progress and consistency. Each small step forward, each task completed, brings you closer to a more organized and fulfilling life.

TAKEAWAYS

1. **Struggle with Time Management:** ADHD often leads to a distorted perception of time, making task management difficult. Dedicate Week Two to support working memory.

2. **Time Audit Worksheet:** Spend one week meticulously tracking all your activities to identify patterns and areas for improvement. This awareness is the first step toward better time management.

3. **Planner for Scheduling:** Spend 5 minutes every evening planning your next day using a physical planner or digital calendar app. Consistent planning helps you use your time efficiently and avoid unexpected disruptions.

4. **Breaking Down Tasks:** Overwhelming tasks become manageable in smaller steps. This technique helps to reduce anxiety and make progress more visible.

5. **Prioritizing with the Eisenhower Matrix:** Categorize tasks based on urgency and importance. This method provides a clear, manageable plan, reducing stress and enhancing productivity.

Chapter 15: Control Anxious Thoughts

The Olympic Swimmer Who Cannot Swim

Federica Pellegrini, one of history's best competitive swimmers, harbors a surprising secret. Born in Mirano, Italy, Pellegrini's ascent to swimming stardom began at a young age. As a teenager, she burst onto the international scene, setting world records and winning medals. Unique achievements adorned her career: she won her first Olympic medal, a silver, at the Athens 2004 Olympics at just 16. In 2008, she became the first woman to break the four-minute barrier in the 400m freestyle at the Beijing Olympics, earning a gold medal and a place in history. Over the years, she has collected numerous World Championship titles and set several world records, making her one of the most decorated swimmers of her generation.

Despite her incredible accomplishments, Pellegrini's relationship with water is complex. Beneath the confident exterior lies a profound unease with deep water. The same element that brought her glory also holds a shadow of fear. Pellegrini admits she feels a sense of dread when swimming in waters where she can't see the bottom. This vulnerability makes her human, reminding us that even the greatest among us grapple with irrational fears. For Pellegrini, this fear isn't just about the physical depth but the unknown that lies beneath. Pellegrini's fear of deep water is a powerful metaphor for the emotional obstacles you might face. Just as she cannot see the bottom of a dark, deep pool, we often cannot see the bottom of our anxieties and fears.

Emotional obstacles are usually irrational yet deeply ingrained. They can hinder your progress and keep you from venturing into new territories in your personal and professional life.

Have you ever felt like your brain is constantly working against you? You're not alone. Your mind can often be a battlefield of negative thoughts and cognitive distortions. A voice in your head that doubts your abilities, amplifies failures and paints every challenge as an insurmountable mountain. This negative self-talk doesn't just erode your self-esteem; it cripples your productivity and makes it difficult to stay motivated. You might find yourself stuck in a cycle of procrastination and self-blame, wondering if you'll ever break free from the mental fog.

You're sitting at your desk, a daunting task before you. Instead of diving in, your mind starts whispering, "You'll never get this done on time. You're not organized enough. What's the point of even trying?" These thoughts swirl around, becoming louder and more convincing with each passing second. The once-manageable task now feels like an insurmountable obstacle. You start to feel overwhelmed, anxious, and stuck. ADHD is not just about distractions; it's about battling an internal dialogue that constantly undermines your confidence and abilities.

Yet, there's hope. This session addresses solutions to overcome the negative self-talk that plagues so many with ADHD. You can challenge and change these automatic negative thoughts with specific tools. This isn't about ignoring reality or pretending everything is perfect. It's about learning to see situations more clearly and respond to them in a healthier, more productive way.

COGNITIVE RESTRUCTURING (W4)

Cognitive Restructuring is a powerful tool designed to help you identify and challenge automatic negative thoughts. Here's how to use it in 6 steps:

1. Write Down Negative Thoughts

    Whenever you think negatively about yourself or your tasks, jot down these thoughts. For example, "I'll never be able to finish this project," or "I'm not good enough for this job."

2. Identify Cognitive Distortions

    Look at your list of negative thoughts and identify the cognitive distortions in each one. Common distortions include overgeneralization (making broad statements based on a single event), catastrophizing (expecting the worst possible outcome), and black-and-white thinking (seeing things in extremes with no middle ground).

3. Challenge the Thoughts

    Report a more realistic, positive alternative for each negative thought. Ask yourself questions like, "Is this thought really true? What evidence do I have? What would I say to a friend in this situation?" Replace "I'll never be able to finish this project" with "I've completed projects before, and I can break this one down into manageable steps."

4. Create Positive Affirmation Cards

    Based on step 3, create positive statements on a set of cards. Examples include "I am capable," "I can manage my time effectively," and "I am resilient." Ensure these affirmations are specific to the areas where you often struggle with negative self-talk.

5. Daily Reading

    Keep these cards handy and read through them daily, especially when you notice negative thoughts creeping in. Reading these positive statements reinforces healthier thought patterns.

6. Repeat Affirmations

    Consistency is key. Repeat these affirmations throughout the day, particularly during self-doubt or stress. This practice can help shift your mindset over time from one of negativity to one of positivity and resilience.

If you apply Cognitive Restructuring, you'll soon notice a change in your mental landscape. Negative thoughts will lose grip, leaving space for a more balanced and realistic perspective. This shift will improve your self-esteem and enhance your ability to tackle tasks with confidence and clarity. You'll be able to manage your time, overcome procrastination, and maintain motivation even in the face of challenges.

As we move to Week 5, you will learn the power of Activation and Motivation. This next session will provide strategies to ignite your drive and sustain your momentum. Get ready to transform your approach to tasks and projects, ensuring that you stay engaged and motivated every step of the way.

TAKEAWAYS

1. **Battling Negative Self-Talk:** Many with ADHD struggle with a constant stream of negative thoughts that undermine their confidence and abilities. Take 10 minutes to write down these thoughts to begin addressing and overcoming them.

2. **Hope Through Cognitive Restructuring:** Cognitive Restructuring helps challenge and change automatic negative thoughts. Spend 15 minutes daily identifying distortions and replacing them with positive affirmations.

3. **Enhancing Self-Esteem and Productivity:** Regularly reading positive affirmations reinforces healthier thought patterns. Dedicate 5 minutes each morning to read through your affirmations.

Chapter 16: Empowering Self-Motivation

Imagine a massive boulder perched precariously at the peak of a towering mountain. It remains motionless for decades, seemingly content in its lofty position. A serene silence surrounds the boulder on the mountain summit. The air is thin and crisp, the sky a boundless expanse of blue, and the landscape below unfolds like a patchwork quilt of greens and browns. Despite its stillness, the boulder has an inherent tension. One day, a sudden shift occurs. Perhaps a tremor in the earth or a gust of wind stronger than usual—something breaks the delicate equilibrium. This is the moment of activation. The boulder begins to move, slowly at first, then gaining speed as gravity takes over. It hurtles down the mountainside, dislodging smaller rocks, kicking up dust, and carving a path through the rugged terrain. This transformation is akin to the power of motivation in a person's life.

When you feel motivated, you can break free from inertia. Like the boulder, your journey starts with a small push—a realization, a goal, or an inspiration. As you move, progress accelerates, momentum builds, and once-insurmountable obstacles are swept aside. The boulder's descent is a tumultuous, exhilarating ride. It crashes through barriers, forges new trails, and leaves a lasting impact on the landscape. Similarly, a motivated person embarks on a dynamic journey, overcoming challenges, creating opportunities, and profoundly influencing the environment. This analogy captures the essence of activation and motivation. It illustrates how a moment of change can unleash a cascade of energy and potential, transforming stillness into action. Similarly, within you lies a dormant force, waiting for the right moment to break free.

If you have ADHD, procrastination is always lurking. Problems with self-motivation, working memory, and planning make tasks and projects overwhelming. However, most of the challenge lies in getting started. In this session, you'll learn activation strategies to help you begin tasks. Additionally, you'll discover ways to sustain motivation, maintain momentum, and progress consistently.

ACTIVATION CHECKLIST (W5)

The Activation Strategies Checklist is a curated list of techniques designed to help you start tasks. Think of it as your go-to manual for overcoming inertia. Some immediately resonate with you, while others require a bit of tweaking. Here are a few examples:

1. Set a timer for 5 minutes
   This technique leverages the Zeigarnik Effect, which posits that you remember uncompleted tasks better than completed ones. Your brain seeks closure and resolution, increasing the likelihood of finishing what you start. Set a timer to work for only 5 minutes. This will reduce the perceived difficulty of starting a task. Once you begin, the Zeigarnik Effect pushes for completion.

2. Focus on the next thing

   Large tasks can be overwhelming. Ask yourself what the very next thing you could accomplish is. For instance, instead of "clean the house," you might break it down into "clean the living room," "vacuum the carpet," and "dust the shelves."

3. Apply visual cues

   Place reminders in strategic locations. Sticky notes on your bathroom mirror or a whiteboard in your office are visual prompts to get started or get back to task.

4. Reward Systems

   Plan small rewards for task completion. Whether it's a short break, a snack, or a few minutes of your favorite activity, knowing there's a reward waiting can be a powerful motivator.

5. Check off Strategies

   As you experiment, note which strategies help you the most. Make a checklist and mark the techniques that you find effective. This personalized list will become a powerful tool in your time management arsenal.

Consistency is key. Make it a habit to use your activation strategies regularly. Over time, initiating tasks will become less daunting as these techniques become second nature.

MOTIVATION TRACKER (W5)

The Motivation Tracker assists you in monitoring and reflecting on your daily motivation levels. It helps you identify patterns and factors that influence your motivation, enabling you to make adjustments.

Here are the 3 points to consider:

1. Rate Your Motivation Level
    At the end of each day, rate your motivation on a scale of 1 to 10. Be honest and reflective in your assessment. This simple act of daily tracking will help you become aware of your motivational states.

2. Take Note
    Keep a journal of factors that impact your motivation. Ask yourself the critical questions. Did you get enough rest? Were you particularly stressed today? Did you eat well and exercise? Where did you spend most of your time? (A cluttered or noisy environment can be distracting and demotivating.)

3. Reflect on Patterns and Adjust
    After tracking for a few weeks, review your entries to identify patterns. You might feel more energized and motivated when you spend time outdoors in the morning. Or when you practice 10 minutes of breathwork soon after waking. Use these insights to adjust your routine and environment. If a tidy workspace boosts your

motivation, make an effort to keep your desk clean. If a specific type of music energizes you, play it during your work sessions.

REWARD SYSTEM (W5)

A Reward System maintains motivation by providing incentives for completing tasks. Rewards act as positive reinforcement, encouraging you to stay on track and complete each step. Choose rewards that genuinely motivate you. These could be simple pleasures like enjoying your favorite snack, taking a short break, or engaging in a fun activity. If you love tea, a cup of your favorite brew can be your reward after completing a step. Then, assign a specific reward to each small step or task completion. This ensures you have something to look forward to as you progress through the task. Finally, ensure compliance and only reward yourself after completing the task. This helps build self-discipline and reinforces the habit of task completion. Promise yourself that you can only have that cup of tea once you complete the planned activity, not a moment before.

These tools boost self-motivation, a crucial element often elusive if you have ADHD. When you properly apply, activate, and sustain motivation strategies, you build a sense of accomplishment that gradually reduces anxiety and boosts confidence. Over time, you will notice reduced procrastination, improved productivity, and higher self-esteem.

By the end of Week 5, you can expect a significant shift in how you approach and manage tasks. You'll notice lower procrastination, higher task initiation, and a deeper understanding of the factors that influence your motivation. This newfound ability to start and sustain tasks will boost your productivity and overall sense of control over your life.

As you continue this journey, remember that each session builds upon the last, creating a comprehensive framework for managing ADHD. Stay committed, stay engaged, and let's move forward with the confidence that you will master your life.

TAKEAWAYS

1. **Overcoming Task Overwhelm:** Problems with self-motivation, working memory, and planning make tasks and projects overwhelming.

2. **Activation Strategies:** This curated list helps you start tasks by overcoming inertia. Practice activation techniques daily to reduce anxiety and boost confidence.

3. **Tracking Motivation:** The Motivation Tracker helps you monitor and reflect on your daily motivation levels. Spend 10 minutes daily rating your motivation and journaling factors that affect it to identify patterns and make adjustments.

4. **Reward System:** Maintaining motivation through rewards provides incentives for task completion. Plan small rewards for finishing tasks to build self-discipline and reinforce good habits.

Chapter 17: Planning Goals You Can Reach

Effective planning is crucial for success in both personal and professional life. However, if you have ADHD, planning can be particularly challenging. Difficulties in maintaining focus, organizing tasks, and managing time hinder effective planning. However, there are many strategies that you can apply to overcome those obstacles. This week you will learn to put together the principles of productivity schools like GTD, PARA, and One Thing. If you follow this process, you are almost guaranteed to complete any project and achieve your goals.

Let's now assemble what you learned during the past five weeks to manage projects, develop goals, and implement a practical plan.

BRAINDUMP

"Your mind is for having ideas, not holding them." - David Allen

Take pen and paper and write down all your projects. Projects have specific deadlines and tasks, which help you to use time and resources better. Consider projects as outputs that you want to produce within a specific date. If projects are outputs, then what are the inputs? What are those things that move a project forward?

There are three.

1. Tasks - Breaking down projects into smaller parts makes the work more accessible to handle and track

2. Meetings - Recap of project challenges and progress discussed

3. Resources - Tools and materials that support the project

Create three folders (Tasks, Meetings, and Resources) to accommodate every project's input. This will help you keep track of progress and quickly retrieve the information needed.

You will notice two main benefits:

1. You will recall ten times more things than expected.

2. Your mind feels light, anxiety disappears, and you gain clarity on the big picture.

THE ART OF SETTING GOALS

With a fresh mind, you can now set goals. While many goal-setting frameworks exist, such as SMART, CLEAR, and HARD, only three principles are crucial. Goals must be:

1. Specific: The goal is unambiguous, providing a precise direction for your efforts.
   Example: Instead of saying, "I want to write a book," specify, "I want to write a 300-page fantasy novel about a young hero's journey to save their kingdom."

2. Measurable: you can track your progress and determine when you've achieved your objective.

Example: Set a measurable target, such as "I will write 1,000 words per day" or "I will complete one chapter every two weeks."

3. Achievable: it's realistic and attainable considering your current resources and constraints.

Example: If you have a full-time job, you are more likely to write for one hour each evening rather than to write for several hours daily.

Furthermore, goals must be big enough to excite you. However, big goals are also scary and overwhelming. This is why you must break them down until you can identify the next optimal step you can take to get closer to your goal. For instance, if you aim to publish a 300-page book in one year, break it down into quarterly, monthly, weekly, and daily goals.

- Yearly: A yearly goal might be to complete the book.

- Quarterly Goals: write 75 pages

- Monthly Goals: write 25 pages

- Weekly Goals: write 6-7 pages

- Daily Goals: write 1 page

If you have ADHD, issues with delayed gratification are pervasive. The problem with long-term goals is that you must complete "trivial" tasks today to (possibly) see the reward months later. However, breaking the project into smaller tasks will keep your motivation high. The boring email to request a research paper today is directly associated with the recognition of publishing a book next year. The once "trivial" activity becomes a clear step toward your highest desires.

FOCUS ON THE MOST IMPACTFUL GOAL

The more goals you set, the less likely you are to achieve any. Instead, focus on the one goal that will have the most significant impact on your life. The best-seller book "The One Thing" by Gary Keller and Jay Papasan perfectly articulates this idea, emphasizing that extraordinary results come from a narrow focus. Each quarter, month, week, and day, ask yourself what one thing if achieved, will bring you closest to your big goal. What is the one thing I can accomplish this quarter that would impact my yearly goal the most? What is the one thing I can accomplish this month that would have the biggest impact on my quarter and, therefore, my yearly goal? Keep on going until you find the most relevant task you can do right now.

This focused approach helps you make substantial progress and avoid overwhelm. By honing in on your most impactful goal, you eliminate distractions and increase the likelihood of success.

EFFECTIVE TIME MANAGEMENT AND TASK SCHEDULING

Once you have goals, projects, and inputs on paper, apply the 2-minute rule and schedule your week. Look at the tasks and complete those that take two minutes or less. If they take longer, schedule them using time blocks. Each time block should have a specific goal and include all related activities.

- Block 1: 8:00 AM - 8:45 AM - Preparation and Planning
  Activity: Review notes and outline for the current chapter.
  Details: Go through the key points to cover in today's writing session; make a brief plan for the session's writing goals.

- Block 2: 9:00 AM - 9:45 AM - Focused Writing
  Activity: Write the first draft of the next section/chapter.
  Details: Write continuously without editing; aim to get the ideas down on paper.

- Block 3: 10:00 AM - 10:45 AM - Continued Writing
  Activity: Continue writing and finish the draft of the current section/chapter.
  Details: Keep writing to complete the initial draft, focusing on maintaining the flow and covering all planned points.

- Block 4: 10:45 AM - 11:00 AM - Review and Outline Next Steps
  Activity: Quick review of writing
  Details: Skim through the draft, note any significant issues or gaps to address later, and outline what to focus on in the next writing session.

SINGLE-TASKING

Research repeatedly shows two things. First, conscious multi-tasking doesn't exist. The brain cannot consciously focus on two things at once. At best, it hops from one to the other (task switching). Second, it takes up to 15 minutes to regain focus on a task. This taxes your working memory, a critical executive function that ADHD already compromises.

Task switching is the process of shifting attention and effort from one task to another. You might tell yourself you are good at it, yet it's often an excuse for novelty needs. Instead, what you're likely to experience when you switch tasks comes in three steps:

1. Constant busy mind

2. Overwhelm

3. Burnout

The problem with task switching is that you always need to re-orient yourself. Your working memory must remember what you were doing and thinking of doing on that task. Due to task-switching inefficiencies, individuals lose about 13 weeks of productivity annually. Therefore, the single-task approach is vital.

For example, if you write in the morning, focus solely on writing. Avoid alternating between blocks of writing, research, and replying to emails. This approach ensures that your brain remains engaged with the task, enhancing creativity and productivity while minimizing the cognitive load associated with task switching.

PRIORITIZE AND EAT THE FROG

You have learned to break down goals and create efficient time blocks. However, you might wonder when to perform specific tasks during the day. First, look at your Eisenhower Matrix (Chapter 14) or any other prioritizing strategy you chose. Then eat the frog.

The idea comes from a quote by Mark Twain: "If it's your job to eat a frog, it's best to do it first thing in the morning. And if it's your job to eat two frogs, it's best to eat the biggest one first." If you complete the most challenging task early on, you can reduce procrastination and build momentum. However, this is not just a quote but also a physiological truth. Norepinephrine, dopamine, and acetylcholine are the molecules of focus, and they peak in the morning.

Here's an option you can follow that seems to find the support of popular productivity schools:

1. Complete anything urgent within the first hour. Removing urgent tasks early in the day will lift a weight from your shoulders.

2. Single task on cognitive taxing activities in the morning. Focus on relevant tasks. If many have the same importance, complete first those that are difficult or boring.

3. Enjoy your day.
    Completing urgent and heavy tasks in the morning will bring peace to your afternoon.

REGULAR REVIEWS AND EVENING PLANNING

Regularly reviewing your progress is essential. Daily and weekly reviews keep motivation high as you see tangible progress and foresee and overcome obstacles. Answer on paper (or digital) the following 3 questions:

- What went well?
- What didn't go well?
- How can I make sure it won't happen again?

With the fresh answers in mind, plan your next day or week.

Plan your day the evening before to avoid losing mental energy in the morning. Remember, your focus in the morning should be on completing the most significant activities. Finally, resist the urge to change your plan the same day unless necessary. Why should you change something you carefully planned just the night before? The answer is often procrastination. Instead, train your brain to stick to the schedule and honor the agreed commitments. You can always adjust the daily review coming up that evening. It's a disciplined approach that helps maintain focus and overcome procrastination.

ACCOUNTABILITY

Finally, consider options like an accountability partner or coach. They can offer timely feedback and encouragement, helping you stay on track and follow through with your commitments. If you have ADHD, this could be even more beneficial. For ADHD, external and immediate consequences are crucial for maintaining focus and motivation. Reporting your progress to an accountability partner or coach provides exactly those consequences.

BRINGING IT ALL TOGETHER

Imagine standing at the edge of a vast forest. Behind you is the path you've traveled, filled with obstacles you've overcome and milestones you've reached. Ahead of you lies an uncharted territory full of potential and possibilities. The tools you've gained during this CBT program are your compass and map, guiding you through this new terrain.

It's important to remember that managing ADHD is an ongoing process. The strategies and techniques you've learned during this program are not one-time fixes but tools to be used continually. Regular self-evaluation and updating of your action plan will help you stay on track and adapt to new challenges. Maintaining motivation can be challenging, especially when progress seems slow. During these times, remind yourself of your achievements and the goals you're working towards. Surround yourself with supportive people who understand your journey and can offer encouragement and guidance.

Finally, embrace the journey. Managing ADHD is not about achieving perfection but about improving continuously and finding what works best for you. Celebrate your successes, learn from your setbacks, and keep moving forward. As you conclude this CBT program, remember that you have the power to shape your future. The self-awareness and skills you've developed are valuable tools that will serve you well in all areas of your life. Use them to build the future you envision, one step at a time.

TAKEAWAYS

1. **Overcoming Planning Challenges:** Effective planning is crucial for success, but ADHD can make it difficult. You can learn to use productivity principles like GTD, PARA, and One Thing to overcome obstacles. Following this structured process helps you achieve your goals.

2. **Braindump:** Spend 15 minutes writing down every task and resource for each project. This process increases recall and reduces anxiety, clarifying the big picture.

3. **The Art of Setting Goals:** Set specific, measurable, and achievable goals. Break down significant goals into smaller tasks to maintain motivation and progress.

4. **Focus on the Most Impactful Goal:** Ask yourself what one thing you can achieve that will have the most significant impact. This focused approach minimizes distractions and increases the likelihood of success. Review and prioritize your goals regularly.

5. **Efficient Time Management and Task Scheduling:** Apply the 2-minute rule and use time blocks for tasks. This structure enhances productivity and task completion.

6. **Single Tasking:** Avoid multitasking to prevent burnout. Focus solely on one task at a time. This approach maintains engagement and enhances creativity.

7. **Prioritize and Eat the Frog:** Complete the most challenging task early in the day to reduce procrastination and build momentum.

8. **Regular Reviews and Evening Planning:** Spend 10 minutes each evening reviewing your progress and planning for the next day. Answer three questions: What went well? What didn't go well? How can I make sure it won't happen again? This habit maintains focus and improves daily productivity.

9. **Accountability:** Consider having an accountability partner or coach. They provide timely feedback and encouragement, helping you stay on track. This external support is especially beneficial for maintaining focus and motivation with ADHD.

Conclusion

As we've explored throughout this book, ADHD in men is a complex and often misunderstood condition that extends far beyond the stereotypical traits of hyperactivity and inattention. For men, ADHD impacts not only how they manage their daily responsibilities but also how they perceive themselves in a society that often demands unwavering focus, consistency, and reliability. It profoundly affects executive functions, self-regulation, and emotional control, influencing nearly every aspect of life, from work to relationships. Understanding ADHD is not just about recognizing these challenges but about adopting strategies and techniques that can transform these obstacles into manageable aspects of life, thereby paving the way for personal and professional success.

Throughout the chapters, we've delved into the nuances of ADHD, from its genetic underpinnings to its manifestation in daily struggles. We have dismantled common misconceptions and provided evidence-based insights into how ADHD affects individuals differently. Key strategies for managing ADHD have been outlined, including the importance of structured routines, cognitive-behavioral techniques, and the potential benefits and risks of medication. We've also highlighted the critical role of self-awareness and emotional regulation in overcoming the challenges posed by ADHD, and how understanding these elements can lead to improved relationships, professional success, and a more fulfilling life.

The journey of understanding and managing ADHD is not just about reducing symptoms but about embracing a new way of living—one that acknowledges the unique challenges and focuses on effective management and growth. By implementing these techniques, men with ADHD can break free from the cycle of frustration and underachievement, moving towards a life filled with greater potential and opportunities. The strategies discussed are not quick fixes, but they represent powerful tools for continuous improvement, enabling you to take control and chart a more fulfilling path forward.

Looking ahead, it's important to recognize that managing ADHD is a continuous journey with immense potential for personal growth. Future research and evolving therapeutic approaches may offer new insights and tools for those living with ADHD. The techniques and strategies shared in this book are a solid foundation, but ongoing adaptation and learning will be key. Embrace the possibilities that lie ahead, as the journey doesn't stop here; it evolves with each new discovery and effort you make.

As you close this book, I encourage you to take the insights and strategies you've learned and apply them to your daily life with enthusiasm and determination. Whether it's refining your time management skills, practicing mindfulness, or seeking professional guidance, every step you take is a powerful move towards greater control and fulfillment. ADHD may be a part of your life, but it does not define you. With the right tools and mindset, you have the potential to create a life of achievement and satisfaction. Your journey is just beginning—embrace it with confidence, courage, and the knowledge that your best days are yet to come.

Thank You

Thank you so much for purchasing my book.

With so many other options available, I truly appreciate you choosing this one. Your support means a lot, and I'm grateful that you took the time to read it all the way to the end.

Before you go, I have a small favor to ask. If you enjoyed the book, **could you please consider posting a review on the platform? Leaving a review is one of the most effective and simplest ways to support independent authors like me.**

Your feedback helps me as an independent author and assists other readers in finding books that might benefit them. Your thoughts would be invaluable in guiding me as I continue to write books that will help you get the results you want. It would mean a lot to me to hear from you.

Use the link or QR code

https://serenitytimelibrary.com/Rev-b0dhv5gxnn

Reference

1. ADHD: The facts. (n.d.). Attention Deficit Disorder Association. Retrieved from https://add.org/adhd-facts/

2. Adler, L. A., Zimmerman, B., Starr, H. L., Silber, S., Palumbo, J., Orman, C., & Spencer, T. (2009). Efficacy and safety of OROS methylphenidate in adults with attention-deficit/hyperactivity disorder: A randomized, placebo-controlled, double-blind, parallel group, dose-escalation study. Journal of Clinical Psychopharmacology, 29(3), 239-247.

3. Alvarez, J. A., & Emory, E. (2006). Executive function and the frontal lobes: A meta-analytic review. Neuropsychology Review, 16(1), 17-42. https://doi.org/10.1007/s11065-006-9002-x

4. American Psychiatric Association. (2013). Diagnostic and statistical manual of mental disorders (5th ed.). American Psychiatric Publishing.

5. Arnsten, A. F. T. (2009). Stress signalling pathways that impair prefrontal cortex structure and function. Nature Reviews Neuroscience, 10(6), 410-422. https://doi.org/10.1038/nrn2648

6. Arnsten, A. F. T. (2011). Catecholamine influences on dorsolateral prefrontal cortical networks. Biological Psychiatry, 69(12), e89-e99. https://doi.org/10.1016/j.biopsych.2011.01.027

7. Basso, J. C., & Suzuki, W. A. (2017). The effects of acute exercise on mood, cognition, neurophysiology, and neurochemical pathways: A review. *Brain Plasticity*, *2*(2), 127–152. https://doi.org/10.3233/BPL-160040

8. Baumeister, R. F., & Heatherton, T. F. (1996). Self-regulation failure: An overview. Psychological Inquiry, 7(1), 1-15.

9. Bijlenga, D., Vollebregt, M. A., Kooij, J. J. S., & Arns, M. (2019). The role of the circadian system in the etiology and pathophysiology of ADHD: Time to redefine ADHD? ADHD Attention Deficit and Hyperactivity Disorders, 11(1), 5-19. https://doi.org/10.1007/s12402-018-0271-z

10. Barkley, R. A. (2015). Emotional dysregulation is a core component of ADHD. In R. A. Barkley (Ed.), Attention-deficit hyperactivity disorder: A handbook for diagnosis and treatment (4th ed., pp. 81-115). The Guilford Press.

11. Bron, T. I., Bijlenga, D., Verduijn, J., et al. (2016). Prevalence of ADHD symptoms across clinical stages of major depressive disorder. Journal of Affective Disorders, 197, 29-35. https://doi.org/10.1016/j.jad.2016.02.053

12. Brown, M. E., & Treviño, L. K. (2006). Ethical leadership: A review and future directions. The Leadership Quarterly, 17(6), 595-616.

13. Bush, G., Valera, E. M., & Seidman, L. J. (2005). Functional neuroimaging of attention-deficit/hyperactivity disorder: A review and suggested future directions.

Biological Psychiatry, 57(11), 1273-1284.
https://doi.org/10.1016/j.biopsych.2005.01.034

14. Center on Addiction. (2019). Prescription drug abuse common among college students, including those at OU. Campus Drug Prevention. Retrieved from https://www.campusdrugprevention.gov/news/prescription-drug-abuse-common-among-college-students-including-those-ou

15. Children and Adults with Attention-Deficit/Hyperactivity Disorder. (n.d.). General prevalence of ADHD. CHADD. https://chadd.org/about-adhd/general-prevalence/

16. Cortese, S., & Vincenzi, B. (2016). Attention-deficit/hyperactivity disorder (ADHD) and obesity: Update 2016. Current Psychiatry Reports, 18(12), 109. https://doi.org/10.1007/s11920-016-0754-1

17. Cutler, A. J. (2022). Adult ADHD: Diagnosis and management. Presented at NEI Congress 2022. Retrieved from https://cdn.neiglobal.com/content/congress/2022/pdf_slides/04_cng/C06_22CNG_AdultADHD_Cutler_Slides.pdf

18. Dalsgaard, S., Østergaard, S. D., Leckman, J. F., Mortensen, P. B., & Pedersen, M. G. (2015). Mortality in children, adolescents, and adults with attention deficit hyperactivity disorder: A nationwide cohort study. The Lancet, 385(9983), 2190-2196. https://doi.org/10.1016/S0140-6736(14)61684-6

19. Diekelmann, S., & Born, J. (2010). The memory function of sleep. Nature Reviews Neuroscience, 11(2), 114-126. https://doi.org/10.1038/nrn2762

20. Duckworth, A. L., & Seligman, M. E. P. (2005). Self-discipline outdoes IQ in predicting academic performance of adolescents. Psychological Science, 16(12), 939-944.

21. Els van der Helm, E., Gujar, N., & Walker, M. P. (2010). Sleep deprivation impairs the accurate recognition of human emotions. Sleep, 33(3), 335-342. https://doi.org/10.1093/sleep/33.3.335

22. Erland, L. A. E., & Saxena, P. K. (2017). Melatonin natural health products and supplements: Presence of serotonin and significant variability of melatonin content. *Journal of Clinical Sleep Medicine, 13*(2), 275-281. https://doi.org/10.5664/jcsm.6462

23. Esteller-Cucala, P., Maceda, I., Børglum, A. D., Demontis, D., Faraone, S. V., Cormand, B., & Lao, O. (2020). Genomic analysis of the natural history of attention-deficit/hyperactivity disorder using Neanderthal and ancient Homo sapiens samples. Scientific Reports, 10(1), 8622. https://doi.org/10.1038/s41598-020-65322-4

24. Faraone, S. V. (2018). The pharmacology of amphetamine and methylphenidate: Relevance to the neurobiology of attention-deficit/hyperactivity disorder and other psychiatric comorbidities. Neuroscience & Biobehavioral Reviews, 87, 255–270. https://doi.org/10.1016/j.neubiorev.2018.02.001

25. Faraone, S. V., & Doyle, A. E. (2001). The nature and heritability of attention-deficit/hyperactivity disorder. Child and Adolescent Psychiatric Clinics, 10(2), 299-316.

26. Faraone, S. V., & Larsson, H. (2019). Genetics of attention deficit hyperactivity disorder. Molecular Psychiatry, 24(4), 562-575.

27. Ferracioli-Oda, E., Qawasmi, A., & Bloch, M. H. (2013). Meta-analysis: Melatonin for the treatment of primary sleep disorders. PLoS One, 8(5), e63773. https://doi.org/10.1371/journal.pone.0063773

28. Fossati, P., Ergis, A. M., & Allilaire, J. F. (2002). Executive functioning in unipolar depression: A review. L'Encéphale, 28(2), 97-107.

29. Froehlich, T. E., Anixt, J. S., Loe, I. M., Chirdkiatgumchai, V., Kuan, L., & Gilman, R. C. (2011). Update on environmental risk factors for attention-deficit/hyperactivity disorder. Current Psychiatry Reports, 13(5), 333-344.

30. Goodman, D. W. (2010). Lisdexamfetamine dimesylate (Vyvanse), a prodrug stimulant for attention-deficit/hyperactivity disorder. P&T, 35(5), 273-277.

31. Hartmann, T. (2019). ADHD: A hunter in a farmer's world (3rd ed.). Healing Arts Press.

32. Hawkey, E., & Nigg, J. T. (2014). Omega-3 fatty acid and ADHD: Blood level analysis and meta-analytic extension of supplementation trials. Clinical Psychology Review, 34(6), 496-505. https://doi.org/10.1016/j.cpr.2014.05.005

33. Hill, E. L. (2004). Executive dysfunction in autism. Trends in Cognitive Sciences, 8(1), 26-32. https://doi.org/10.1016/j.tics.2003.11.003

34. Huberman, A. (2023). Why is morning sunlight important? Huberman Lab. Retrieved from https://ai.hubermanlab.com/s/Ns8bG2uQ

35. Johnson, R. J., Gold, M. S., Johnson, D. R., Ishimoto, T., Lanaspa, M. A., Zahniser, N. R., & Avena, N. M. (2011). Attention-deficit/hyperactivity disorder: Is it time to reappraise the role of sugar consumption? Postgraduate Medicine, 123(5), 39-49. https://doi.org/10.3810/pgm.2011.09.2458

36. Kadlaskar, G., Piergies, A., & Miller, M. (2023). Environmental risk factors for attention-deficit/hyperactivity disorder. In Clinical handbook of ADHD assessment and treatment across the lifespan (pp. 209-242). Springer.

37. Kenworthy, L., Yerys, B. E., Anthony, L. G., & Wallace, G. L. (2008). Understanding executive control in autism spectrum disorders in the lab and in the real world. Neuropsychology Review, 18(4), 320-338. https://doi.org/10.1007/s11065-008-9077-7

38. Landolt, H. P. (2008). Sleep homeostasis: A role for adenosine in humans? Biochemical Pharmacology, 75(11), 2070-2079. https://doi.org/10.1016/j.bcp.2008.02.024

39. Michelson, D., Faries, D., Wernicke, J., Kelsey, D., Kendrick, K., Sallee, F. R., Spencer, T., & Greenhill, L. (2002). Atomoxetine in the treatment of children and

adolescents with ADHD: A randomized, placebo-controlled, dose-response study. Pediatrics, 108(5), E83. https://doi.org/10.1542/peds.108.5.e83

40. Mischel, W., Ebbesen, E. B., & Zeiss, A. R. (1972). Cognitive and attentional mechanisms in delay of gratification. Journal of Personality and Social Psychology, 21(2), 204-218. https://doi.org/10.1037/h0032198

41. Mischel, W., Shoda, Y., & Rodriguez, M. I. (1989). Delay of gratification in children. Science, 244(4907), 933-938.

42. Moffitt, T. E., et al. (2011). A gradient of childhood self-control predicts health, wealth, and public safety. Proceedings of the National Academy of Sciences, 108(7), 2693-2698.

43. National Institute of Mental Health. (n.d.). Attention-deficit/hyperactivity disorder (ADHD). National Institutes of Health. https://www.nimh.nih.gov/health/statistics/attention-deficit-hyperactivity-disorder-adhd

44. Nehlig, A. (1999). Are we dependent upon coffee and caffeine? A review on human and animal data. Neuroscience & Biobehavioral Reviews, 23(4), 563-576. https://doi.org/10.1016/S0149-7634(98)00050-5

45. Nikolas, M. A., & Burt, S. A. (2010). Genetic and environmental influences on ADHD symptom dimensions of inattention and hyperactivity: A meta-analysis. Journal of Abnormal Psychology, 119(1), 1-17.

46. Petrowski, K., Bührer, S., & Albus, C. (2020). Increase in cortisol concentration due to standardized bright

and blue light exposure on saliva cortisol in the morning following sleep laboratory. Stress, 24(1), 29-35. https://doi.org/10.1080/10253890.2020.1741543

47. Pelsser, L. M., Frankena, K., Toorman, J., Savelkoul, H. F., Dubois, A. E., Pereira, R. R., & Buitelaar, J. K. (2011). Effects of a restricted elimination diet on the behaviour of children with attention-deficit hyperactivity disorder (INCA study): A randomised controlled trial. The Lancet, 377(9764), 494-503. https://doi.org/10.1016/S0140-6736(10)62227-1

48. Psychology Today. (2020). Stimulants and autism. Retrieved from Psychology Today website.

49. Shoda, Y., Mischel, W., & Peake, P. K. (1990). Predicting adolescent cognitive and self-regulatory competencies from preschool delay of gratification: Identifying diagnostic conditions. Developmental Psychology, 26(6), 978-986.

50. Silberman, E. K., Reus, V. I., Calabrese, J. R., Bond, D. J., El-Mallakh, R. S., Findling, R. L., ... & Wingo, A. P. (2017). Use of stimulants in bipolar disorder. Current Psychiatry Reports. Retrieved August 5, 2024, from https://link.springer.com/article/10.1007/s11920-017-0758-x

51. Smith, E. (2022, January 4). Do stimulants work for treatment-resistant depression? HealthyPlace. Retrieved August 5, 2024, from https://www.healthyplace.com/depression/depression-treatment/do-stimulants-work-for-treatment-resistant-depression

52. Smith, J. (2022). The impact of ADHD medications on depression. Journal of Mental Health Studies, 29(3), 215-230.

53. Tai, X. Y., Chen, C., Manohar, S., & Husain, M. (2022). Impact of sleep duration on executive function and brain structure. Communications Biology, 5(1), 201. https://doi.org/10.1038/s42003-022-03123-3

54. Van Emmerik-van Oortmerssen, K., van de Glind, G., Koeter, M. W., Allsop, S., Auriacombe, M., Barta, C., ... & van den Brink, W. (2012). Prevalence of attention-deficit hyperactivity disorder in substance use disorder patients: A meta-analysis and meta-regression analysis. Drug and Alcohol Dependence, 122(1-2), 11-19. https://doi.org/10.1016/j.drugalcdep.2011.12.007

55. Volkow, N. D., Wang, G. J., Fowler, J. S., & Ding, Y. S. (2005). Imaging the effects of methylphenidate on brain dopamine: New model on its therapeutic actions for attention-deficit/hyperactivity disorder. Biological Psychiatry, 57(11), 1410-1415.

56. Volkow, N. D., Wang, G. J., Kollins, S. H., Wigal, T. L., Newcorn, J. H., Telang, F., ... & Swanson, J. M. (2009). Evaluating dopamine reward pathway in ADHD: Clinical implications. JAMA, 302(10), 1084-1091. https://doi.org/10.1001/jama.2009.1308

57. Watkins, E., & Brown, R. G. (2002). Rumination and executive function in depression: An experimental study. Journal of Neurology, Neurosurgery & Psychiatry, 72(3), 400-402.

58. Young, S., Moss, D., Sedgwick, O., Fridman, M., & Hodgkins, P. (2015). A meta-analysis of the prevalence of attention deficit hyperactivity disorder in incarcerated populations. Psychological Medicine, 45(2), 247-258. https://doi.org/10.1017/S0033291714000762

59. Zeitzer, J. M., Dijk, D. J., Kronauer, R., Brown, E., & Czeisler, C. A. (2000). Sensitivity of the human circadian pacemaker to nocturnal light: Melatonin phase resetting and suppression. Journal of Physiology, 526(3), 695-702. https://doi.org/10.1111/j.1469-7793.2000.00695.x

Made in the USA
Monee, IL
21 December 2024

74919266R00104